# LORD
## OF
# SONG

# LORD OF SONG

## THE MESSIAH REVEALED IN THE PSALMS

## RONALD B. ALLEN
### FOREWORD BY GEORGE BEVERLY SHEA

MULTNOMAH · PRESS

Portland, Oregon 97266

Cover design and illustration by Larry Ulmer
Edited by Steve Halliday

LORD OF SONG
© 1985 by Multnomah Press
Portland, Oregon 97266

Printed in the United States of America

**Library of Congress Cataloging-in-Publication Data**

Allen, Ronald Barclay.
  Lord of song.

    1. Bible.   O.T.   Psalms—Criticism, interpretation,
etc.   2. Messiah—Prophecies.   3. Typology (Theology)
I. Title.
BB1430.2.A345     1985        223'.2064        85-21693
ISBN 0-88070-129-3 (pbk.)

85  86  87  88  89  90  –  10  9  8  7  6  5  4  3  2  1

To my mother,
Vantoria Allen—
For all you have taught me
regarding the Savior's Song!

# CONTENTS

Foreword ........................................................... 9
Introduction ..................................................... 11

## PART ONE: Y'SHUA—THE CENTER OF THE SCRIPTURES

Chapter 1    Walking with Y'shua ................................. 15
Chapter 2    Y'shua and the Scriptures ......................... 21
Chapter 3    Y'shua and the Psalms ............................. 35

## PART TWO: Y'SHUA—THE SINGER OF THE PSALMS

Chapter 4    Body Song ......................................... 43
Chapter 5    Teacher's Song .................................... 57
Chapter 6    Shepherd's Song ................................... 71
Chapter 7    Passover Song ..................................... 87
Chapter 8    Passion Song ...................................... 103
Chapter 9    Resurrection Song ................................. 119
Chapter 10   Triumph Song ...................................... 131

## PART THREE: THE SONGS WE SING TO Y'SHUA

Chapter 11   The Beauty of Song ................................ 149
Chapter 12   The Song of My Father ............................. 157
Chapter 13   So Let's Join the Song! ........................... 175

# FOREWORD

*I Found a Friend
when life seemed not worth living.
I Found a Friend
so tender and forgiving . . .*

**I**'m not sure how many times I've sung those comforting words in evangelistic crusades across the world with the Billy Graham team. I lost count long ago. But I do know that wherever hungry ears have ached to hear of and believe in the love and grace of a faithful God, that song has had a mighty impact. The song speaks to everyone, it seems, and I am so grateful for the privilege of bringing to people its tender words.

One thing has bothered me a little, however. I believe that I have never given Roc Hillman—the lyricist who put those comforting words to Barclay Allen's music—his proper due. Perhaps now I can partly make up for that.

I have been singing I *Found a Friend* regularly since 1953. It has been used in countless crusades, on TV programs, and in our own concerts of sacred song. And like many great songs and hymns of the church, there is a story behind the song. That story, tender and beautiful, is told in this book by Barclay Allen's son, Ronald. It is *very* touching to me and it will reach hearts in a hurry.

But as tender and touching as that story is, it is not the heart of this book—*Jesus* is. The story of Barclay Allen's conversion is just one example of how the Lord of Song, Jesus Christ, can change and mold and reshape stubborn human hearts for his glory . . . so that his redeemed children can join their voices in a joyous and never-ending song of praise to our great and wonderful Savior.

*That* is the message of this book. As you read, I trust that your heart will be warmed and enriched as mine has been. And I hope you too have found the Lord of Song, Jesus Christ, to be *your* friend.

George Beverly Shea

# INTRODUCTION

**H**undreds of years ago Saint Augustine called the Lord Jesus Christ *iste cantator psalmorum*, "He, the singer of the psalms." This book is about the Savior and the psalms that he sang. *Jesus is Lord of Song*.

Moishe Rosen has startled many people by his arresting phrasing, particularly the name of the missionary outreach he heads, Jews for Jesus. He has more recently caused us to examine more fully the Jewishness of Jesus by saying, " *Y'shua* is the Jewish way to say 'Jesus'." Because this book is so centered on the Hebrew hymnal which became the libretto of the Savior, I will often use the Jewish name Y'shua as well.

This book is not a technical treatise. It is written to be read and enjoyed. The argumentation that undergirds my interpretations of these psalms will soon (please, Lord!) be available in my commentary on the psalms.

My hope is that you will enjoy the book even without the commentary! I hope as well that you will appreciate more fully than ever the wonder of our Savior, Y'shua of Nazareth, who loved the psalms so much.

This book is very personal, as you will see. It concludes with the story of my father, the late Barclay Allen. He was a gifted musician who came at long last to sing the song of the Savior who had become his friend.

As you read this book, my prayer is that Y'shua, Lord of Song, will become your dearest friend as well.

In the Shalom of Y'shua the Messiah.

And now, to the song . . .

# PART ONE

# Y'shua
# The Center
# of the
# Scriptures

# 1

# Walking
# with
# Y'shua

**I**t was the afternoon of the first Easter. Two distressed, puzzled men were on their way to their home town of Emmaus. As they walked they talked. They talked as people talk who are overwhelmed by events they do not understand, but which have affected them profoundly. Their talking was a release from the swirling tide of emotion and confusion within. Sometimes they both spoke at once. For moments they were silent. Then one would speak again.

"Why?"

"What does it all mean?"

"And what about the rumors from the women?"

They talked as survivors talk after a volcano erupts or a flood subsides. They rehearsed over and over what they knew, where they had been, how they had fared. Most of all, they wondered what it all meant.

They talked as friends talk who have lost a companion. They talked as soldiers who have lost a champion. They talked as a people who had lost their king.

## A Stranger Comes

They were scarcely aware of the third man who joined them on the road. He just seemed to appear as they were walking together.

His question seemed absurd. All at once he asked, "What are you discussing together as you walk along?"

Surely he could not be serious! They looked at each other incredulously, but they didn't really look at him. One of them, Cleopas, said, "Are you the only one living in Jerusalem who doesn't know the things that have happened there in these days?"

He seemed still not to know. It was as though he'd been in a cave or lost in the desert; perhaps he had just washed ashore from a shipwreck.

The stranger pressed on and asked, "What things?"

With another look at each other, the two told him. They took it as another chance to set things right in their own minds. As they talked—first one, then the other—they pieced together what little they knew and what they didn't know. They barely looked at their companion. He was just a new excuse to continue their discussion and to work through their sorrow.

They told him of Y'shua of Nazareth and how wonderful he had been. They told him of how he had spoken. In his words and in his manner there had been something of the mystery of God. They told him how it had seemed, after so many generations, at last there had come a prophet of God again in Israel. They told him of how he had been, what he had been like. No one had ever spoken like him. And his deeds—his deeds were like his words. There had been the power of God in this man. And people who knew God . . . ah, they had seen God in him.

They reported how others had reacted against him. They had been jealous of his power, fearful of his presence, distressed over his person. Priests and religious rulers had conspired for his death.

"They crucified the one we thought might have been the promised one of the ages, the redeemer of Israel!"

Then in a rush they told him the strangest thing of all:

"Now, today, some of the women who loved him have started some crazy stories," one said. "They went to the tomb early this morning but the body was gone."

"Instead of his body, they said they saw angels," said the other.

"And the angels said he was alive!"

"Some checked the tomb and found it open and empty."

"But none saw him."

These were the things they said to the stranger who walked along with them that afternoon.

## The Stranger Speaks

Have you ever wondered what it must have been like to have been one of those two men?

Here were two people who had believed that Y'shua of Nazareth might have been the Messiah of Israel. They had been in Jerusalem when he had been put to death as a criminal against the state and a blasphemer against Yahweh. Then they had heard strange rumors of angelic visions and that he might again be alive.

But as for them, they had had enough. It had all been quite too much. They were on their way home from the Passover festival that had ended so badly.

Then a stranger joined them. He asked questions and reacted strongly to their reply. He said they were foolish and slow to believe. He flabbergasted them by insisting they should have understood these things. All of these events, he said, were so clear, so obvious, so expected. All these things had been spoken by the prophets long ago.

These were his very words:

> "How foolish you are, and how slow of heart to believe all that the prophets have spoken! Did not the Messiah have to suffer these things and then enter his glory?" (Luke 24:25- 26).

Then he took them through the Hebrew Scriptures, beginning with Moses and all the prophets, and told them everything that had been said concerning himself.

## Dreams of a Warp in Time

Years ago when I was a student in college I had a wonderful professor of history for the freshman course in "Western Civ." She had been the first woman to join the history department of my college. In a male-dominated discipline she had surpassed all other contenders for the position.

The chairman ruefully accepted her into his department. Later he learned to cherish her.

This teacher had a consummate love for history. Her lectures were always in the present tense; history was alive for her.

Her last question of the final exam for the first semester had a three-part, subjective element: "If you could go through a time warp and be an observer (but not a participant!) in any three events in ancient history, what would these be, and why?"

Most, I suppose, wrote about the battles of Salamis or Thermopylae. Some would have liked to have been in the theater for the first performance of a play by Aristophanes, or perhaps to have sat in the Coliseum in Rome to watch gladiators fight (or lions maul Christians!). Some wished they could have been in the room when Socrates drank his poison or in a class when Plato taught.

My three desires were a bit different. They remain unchanged. My time-warp dreams all relate to the Scriptures:

- To have hidden in the folds of Moses's cloak when the glory of Yahweh passed by.
- To have huddled with the women beneath the cross when the Savior died.
- To have walked with the two disciples on the road to Emmaus when the resurrected Lord explained the meaning of the Hebrew Bible.

And if my choice were limited to one, it would be the last. This must have been the most stunning lecture in the history of learning.

Move over Walter Kaiser! Out of the way Elmer Martens and Bruce Waltke! Who would need Gerhard von Rad or Walther Eichrodt! What it must have been to have heard the Lord himself explain the inner meaning and ongoing purpose of his word concerning himself. Ah, to have been walking along with those men and to have heard that voice!

**The Guest Is Host**

The men did not discover who had been with them until they were about to eat. They had urged the stranger to stay with them in their home, for the day was past and the travelers were weary. Although he was a guest at their table, it was he who took the bread, gave thanks to God, and then broke it and held it out to them.

All at once, it was clear to the two men.

- It is he!
- It is all true!
- He *is* alive!

And there he was holding out bread for them to eat; a sacrament was extended at their table by the risen Y'shua!

As soon as they recognized him, he disappeared. He who had walked and talked with them and had held out bread to them was gone. But it had been no mirage. No dream. It had really been he. *Y'shua is alive!*

**Burning Hearts**

And all along the road he had been holding out bread for them to eat—the bread of life. The true meaning of the Word of God. They said to one another,

> Were not our hearts burning within us while he talked with us on the road and opened the Scriptures to us? (Luke 24:32).

Though it was nearly dark they set off at once for Jerusalem. There they found the Eleven and the others with them. The whole room scintillated with the news: It is true! The Lord is alive! He had appeared to Simon. And these two witnesses added their amazing testimony!

**They Should Have Known**

There is something even more amazing than the facts of this narrative: it is the attitude of our risen Lord toward the two disciples from Emmaus. *He said that they should have known!* By their failure to understand, he marked them as foolish and slow of heart to believe.

He maintained that the Hebrew prophets had described the suffering and glorification of the Promised One. All one had to do to understand the events of those days was to know the prophets.

Yet to know the prophets was not an easy task. The prophets speak of a royal deliverer who would be a king greater than David. The prophets speak as well of a priest who will be more wonderful than Aaron. And the prophets speak of a servant who will suffer and die for the sins of the people.

Some of the Jews of the day were confused—and well they might be! Was Elijah to come before the Promised One? Was the Coming One to be a prophet or a teacher? And when he comes, how will we know him?

Remember the confusion that attended the preaching of John the Baptist? Some came to him and asked if he were the Messiah. Then they asked if he were Elijah or the Prophet (John 1:19-21). These questions show the people were confused and uncertain. They were living in an age of great expectancy, but they were quite unsure as to what or whom to expect.

Many scholars believe that the Jewish sectarians in the Qumran community near the Dead Sea were looking for more than one Messiah. The questions that had come to both John and Y'shua showed the puzzlement of the people.

Today we look back and say, "Yes, they should have known!"

I wonder, though. If we were there, would we have known any better?

It is in part the purpose of this book to see what they might have known. It is also a very real purpose of this book to learn some of the things we may know today concerning the teaching of the Hebrew Scriptures about the coming of the one whose name is Y'shua.

But wouldn't it have been something to have been on that walk and to have learned it first from him?

# 2

# Y'shua and the Scriptures

The two disciples from Emmaus rushed back to Jerusalem. There they found the Eleven and the others who were with them. These friends of Y'shua were ecstatic with joy. Simon had seen the risen Lord! The rumors were true! The Lord indeed was risen from the grave!

Then the two from Emmaus added their story of how he had appeared to them as they were walking to their town. How they must have laughed and wept as they told of this encounter and then of his revelation to them at the table.

"As soon as we knew who he was, he was gone!"

## He Appears

And then he appeared again.

*There he was!* He had come out of nowhere.

His words were the traditional Jewish greeting, "Peace to you." He said to them, "Shalom." But never had the Hebrew word *shalom* meant so much.

Despite his words, the suddenness of his appearance terrified them. Though they had been speaking of his resurrection, they supposed him to be a spirit.

His words came to comfort and encourage. "Cease to doubt," he said. "Look and touch, and be believing." No spirit had flesh and bones as the one who stood and spoke to them.

Still they were fearful, not daring to believe their eyes nor trust their ears. Then he asked if they had anything to eat.

Someone handed to him a serving of fish.

He ate.

He who had died and had been buried ate fish and honey before them.

This was no ghost! This was the Lord of glory!

## He Speaks

And then he spoke:

This is what I told you while I was still with you: Everything must be fulfilled that was written about me in the Law of Moses, the Prophets and the Psalms (Luke 24:44).

Then to all of them he explained again the central meaning of the Hebrew Scriptures. He explained how the facts of his suffering and resurrection were fully anticipated in the Bible. It is just that they had missed the clues. They had not gotten the message.

One of the repeated teachings of Y'shua is that people should have understood that the Scriptures speak constantly of him.

## Y'shua and Nicodemus

Think back to the famous encounter between our Lord and the learned Jewish scholar Nicodemus (John 3). I suppose this chapter is one of the most well-known texts in the Bible. Yet we still have lessons to learn from it.

Nicodemus was a Hebrew scholar of the first rank. He was a Pharisee and a member of the Sanhedrin. He had heard the words of Jesus and had seen his acts when the Lord brusquely took command in the temple, driving out merchandisers during the holy feast of Passover.

## In the Night

Nicodemus came to Y'shua by night for an interview. In the Gospel of John the words "day and night" and "light and dark" are used in special ways. These words describe not only physical features but spiritual realities. Nicodemus came to Y'shua in the darkness, for he was not yet ready to commit himself to the Lord openly. His boldness came later. After Jesus died, Nicodemus was one of those who helped bury the Lord's body. At that time, John reminds us, this was the same Nicodemus who had first come to Y'shua by night (John 19:39).

In fact, it was at the end of the interview with Nicodemus (John 3:19-21) that Y'shua spoke of the demand—for him and others like him who desire to have favor with God—to come out into the light. To remain in the darkness is to continue in sin. Since the light has come into the world, those who do the truth must come to the light. Light and dark are principal issues of the interview between our Lord and the great scholar Nicodemus. As we shall see, these are not the only physical/spiritual realities in this text.

But the amazing thing was that Nicodemus came to Y'shua at all. For a man of his standing and station to interview an itinerant preacher from Galilee would be like the dean of Harvard Law School asking for legal pointers from a New York cabbie.

But he came, nonetheless. He had heard in that voice and witnessed in that person the undeniable mark of the presence of God. So even though he came to Jesus by cover of darkness, he did come.

## Be Born Again?

You remember Y'shua's startling words to Nicodemus. It was to him that Y'shua insisted that one must be born again in order to see the kingdom of God.

The response of Nicodemus was properly incredulous. Y'shua regularly brought out that response in people! He was, as Thomas Howard phrased, *Christ the Tiger.*

Nicodemus said, "How may a person be born a second time when he is old? Surely you do not expect a person to crawl back inside his mother's womb!"

Y'shua seemed to answer these questions with new riddles. He insisted that his first challenge was correct. Only by being born a second time may a person see the kingdom of God. But then Y'shua began to differentiate between the nature of the two births he was describing:

> I tell you the truth, unless a man is born of water and the Spirit, he cannot enter the kingdom of God. Flesh gives birth to flesh, but the Spirit gives birth to spirit (John 3:5-6).

These words have continued to trouble readers through the ages. Not only Nicodemus was stunned by them. But I think Jesus was being quite consistent as he pressed on concerning the two births that the kingdom of God demands as a passport for entry.

The first birth is the natural birth of the physical body, the physical passage of the flesh from the watery environment of the womb. The second birth is spiritual, a work of the Spirit of God distinct from the birth of the flesh. The second birth is from above; for the phrase "born again" may also mean "born from above."

- Water birth is the birth of the flesh.
- Spirit birth is the birth of the Spirit.

**Wind and Spirit**

Y'shua then began to speak of wind, for the Spirit is like the wind. The Greek word *pneuma* may be translated both "wind" and "spirit." In the shift from "spirit" to "wind," our Lord was using a delicious pun, so characteristic of Jewish culture.

The wind is like the Spirit, for it is a power whose effects we can observe but cannot adequately predict or control:

> The wind blows wherever it pleases. You hear its sound, but you cannot tell where it comes from or where it is going. So it is with everyone born of the Spirit (John 3:8).

These words, familiar to us by repeated reading, were new concepts when Nicodemus first heard them. They assaulted his senses. They crashed against his learning. His head swam with the sound of them. He asked how such things could possibly be.

Y'shua's response was that he should have known all

of these things! In fact, Y'shua speaks almost condescendingly of the credentials of Nicodemus. He asked, "Are you truly a scholar and you do not know these things? Are you really a bona fide professor of Hebrew Scripture, and you do not understand?" It is almost as though the Lord is about to ask Nicodemus to produce his diploma! Could mail-order, bogus schools have existed so long ago?

**Things of the Heavens**

In a sense, Y'shua seems almost exasperated as he says to Nicodemus, "How may I ever tell you heavenly things if you do not understand and believe these earthly things?"

And now Y'shua speaks the most startling words of all. Most of us have never stopped to listen well to these words. We are so anxious to get to the words of the gospel in verses 16-17 and the words of condemnation in verses 18-21, we tend to rush over the words of mystery in verses 13-15.

Here they are. Read these words slowly and thoughtfully:

No one has ever gone into heaven except the one who came from heaven—the Son of Man. Just as Moses lifted up the snake in the desert, so the Son of Man must be lifted up, that everyone who believes in him may have eternal life (John 3:13-15).

These verses present three profound developments of the Hebrew Scriptures. Perhaps it was this sort of thing that the Lord explained more fully after his resurrection. Yet he expected that Nicodemus would be able to figure out these things and to find in them his own pathway to the light of God in Y'shua.

Here are the three elements:

- The Messianic title "Son of Man."
- The sign of the serpent in the wilderness.
- The riddle of heavenly ascending and descending.

Let's look at these in some detail.

## Son of Man

Jesus adopted the phrase "Son of Man" to describe himself and his messianic purpose. Biblical scholars continue to debate the origin and meaning of this phrase, but I believe the Old Testament gives us sufficient clues to help us understand. To discover the meaning of the phrase "the Son of Man" we need to turn back to the Book of Daniel.

(The expression "son of man" is used some ninety times in the book of Ezekiel, always in cases where God is speaking to his prophet [see for example, Ezekiel 2:3, "Son of man, I am sending you to the Israelites, . . ."] The point of this phrase in Ezekiel seems to be that Ezekiel was but the human agent for the divine message. The prophet was not to think of himself as the originator of the message, only its spokesman. It is in the book of Daniel that we seem to find the Old Testament basis for the use that our Lord makes of the phrase "son of man" rather than the book of Ezekiel.)

The Book of Daniel has two distinct parts. Chapters 1-6 are filled with Daniel's interaction with kings and emperors. It is in these chapters that we find the great stories of Daniel and his Jewish friends in the courts of Nebuchadnezzar, Belshazzar, and Darius.

Chapters 7-12 of Daniel are significantly different in tone and content. These chapters contain extensive reports of the prophetic dreams and visions of Daniel. These latter chapters are "apocalyptic," filled with symbol, mystery, imagination, and intrigue.

## Image and Beasts

Daniel 7 gives the Old Testament basis for the phrase "Son of Man" as a messianic title. The chapter recasts the same basic message as presented in Daniel 2, but with new imagery and a different tone. Daniel 2 gives us the dream image of Nebuchadnezzar, a multi-layered metal statue that speaks of the nations that will rule over the people of God until the time of the end and the coming of the smashing stone that leads to the kingdom of God.

Daniel 7 speaks of the same concepts but in terms of fantastic beasts rather than as different metals composing a statue. The four beasts of the chapter symbolize the same nations as the four metals of chapter 2.

- The beast like a lion (Daniel 7:4) is the same as the head of gold (Daniel 2:32, 37), representing Babylon.
- The beast like a bear (Daniel 7:5) is the same as the chest of silver (Daniel 2:32, 39), representing Medo-Persia.
- The beast like a leopard (Daniel 7:6) is the same as the trunk and thighs of bronze (Daniel 2:32, 39), representing Greece.
- The nondescript, terrible beast (Daniel 7:7) is the same as the legs of iron (Daniel 2:33, 40), representing Rome.
- The little horn speaking arrogant things (Daniel 7:8) is from the same setting as the toes mixed of iron and clay (Daniel 2:33, 41-43), representing the man of sin, the beast, who will arise in the latter period of human history to blaspheme God and torment his people (Revelation 13:1-10).

## Here Comes the Judge

Then comes the end.

Then comes the judge.

Then comes the kingdom of God.

Daniel 2 describes a stone cut without hands that strikes the image of human government, smashes it fully, and becomes God's kingdom (Daniel 2:35, 44-45). This kingdom shall never be destroyed. It is a kingdom established not by man, but by God; here is a kingdom established not for evil, but for good.

Daniel 7 looks at this great transfer of power from a heavenly perspective, describing the new kingdom from above.

Daniel's vision of the most holy God has within it all of the grandeur and awesomeness of the vision of the prophet Isaiah (Isaiah 6:1-13), and all the mystery, symbol, and wonder of the vision of the prophet Ezekiel (Ezekiel 1:1-3:15).

Daniel saw into highest heaven. There he saw holy God (Daniel 7:9-14). He saw the arrangements of thrones and the seating of the Ancient of Days. His view of God the Father is remarkable. He speaks of the whiteness of his garment and his hair like wool. His throne was of fire, with burning wheels. A fiery stream flashed out before him, and innumerable angels ministered to him.

Books were brought and were opened.

And all the while, on earth below, an arrogant, boastful beast was speaking. But then the beast was slain and delivered to the fire.

Who was the slayer? Who the victor?

Daniel says he saw him coming:

> In my vision at night I looked, and there before me was one like *a son of man*, coming with the clouds of heaven. He approached the Ancient of Days and was led into his presence. He was given authority, glory and sovereign power; all peoples, nations and men of every language worshiped him. His dominion is an everlasting dominion that will not pass away, and his kingdom is one that will never be destroyed (Daniel 7:13-14).

## Son of Man/Son of God

Who then is the Son of Man? He is the victor over the beast at the end of time. He is the one who comes to the Ancient of Days to receive the kingdom of God and the praise of all his people. He is King of kings and Lord of lords. He is the Promised One of the ages.

When Jesus used this term concerning himself, it was a bold claim on his part to be the Promised One of the ages, the one who would be the final deliverer from all human pain and suffering The phrase speaks of the heavenly court, of the victory of the ages, of eternal glory.

The term also suggests the mystery of the Incarnation. From our perspective, the amazing thing about Y'shua of Nazareth is that he, a man, was truly God. Perhaps we may say that from the perspective of deity, the amazing thing was that he, truly God, was now truly man.

That is, the phrase *the Son of Man* speaks of the final battle and the coming of God's kingdom. It declares as well the identification of Y'shua with mankind. For he who was of old became flesh; very God became very man. He who has lived forever became born of a woman, a descendant of Adam.

Hence, when Jesus identified himself as "the Son of Man" to Nicodemus, he was making stunning claims for himself—claims worthy of Nicodemus's early assessment that he was truly a man from God (John 3:2).

## Angel's Bread

A second element in the self-disclosure of Y'shua to Nicodemus came from the Torah of Moses. The words of Jesus concerning the snake take us back to the time that Israel was wandering in the wilderness.

But what an unexpected association he makes of himself to the snake in the desert! One of the last rebellious acts the people of the wilderness community committed against Yahweh and his servant Moses was on their way to Edom. As had happened so often in the past, the people became discouraged with their harsh life in the desert, and as before, they complained that Moses should have left them in Egypt to die rather than to die in the unbearable wilderness. Food and water were scarce and the people hated the detestable bread.

Worthless bread? It was manna from heaven the people contemned. Manna, the daily miracle of God's provision. Manna, the mark of his grace. Manna, gift of his love.

Listen to the way manna is described by the writer of Psalm 78:

> Yet he gave a command to the skies above
>> and opened the doors of the heavens;
> he rained down manna for the people to eat,
>> he gave them the grain of heaven.
> Men ate the bread of angels;
>> he sent them all the food they could eat
>> (Psalm 78:23-25).

Think of it! At the command of Yahweh the heavens, which normally obey his command to give rain upon the earth, were now dripping with the grain of heaven. Men were able to eat the bread of angels! Today we make angel food cake with lots of egg whites. Back then it was made with manna!

But the people, in an all-too-human way, had turned on God's gift because of its very regularity. Can't you hear a husband say, "What's for dinner?" His wife responds, "Manna loaf." Yesterday it was fried manna, tomorrow it will be boiled manna. How many ways can one serve manna? Can one make a manna quiche? What about manna pizza? Banana manna?

But the point of manna was that it was a miracle food, proceeding from God's grace, in a place where there was no other food. God's daily gift of manna was a continual reminder of the dependence of the people upon Yahweh.

Manna was a special food. Some have thought it is a naturally occurring secretion of insects in the desert. But manna was unnatural, unknown, uncommon. It was a new work of God for the special feeding of his people in a wilderness land. In fact, the very Hebrew word *mannah* means, "What is it?"

Moses explained this to the community in his last great oration:

> He humbled you, causing you to hunger and then feeding you with manna, which neither you nor your fathers had known, to teach you that man does not live on bread alone but on every word that comes from the mouth of the LORD (Deuteronomy 8:3).

It was this manna that the people contemned. In their contempt for manna they showed contempt for Yahweh. In spurning his gift of food, they spurned his daily grace.

### Contemptible Snakes

God caused them great grief by bringing into their midst venomous snakes which caused a terrible plague among the people. Since they had turned from his blessing, calling it contemptible, God brought genuine contempt into their lives in the form of noxious snakes.

Then, in an abrupt and surprising manner, God had Moses make a bronze image of one of those detestable snakes and hold it high on a pole. Whoever would look at that snake image on the pole would be spared from painful death by the snake venom.

They had contemned God's gift; he made an object of contempt the only means for their life.

### Contemptible Savior!

*Y'shua compared himself to that bronze serpent!*

Jesus predicted his death by these words. He pointed to a time when he would be held up as an object of contempt. He who knew no sin would be held high in ignominy. But all who would look to him would live.

See how it is? In his words to Nicodemus, early on in his ministry, our Lord said it all. And he said it from the texts of the Hebrew Bible.

### Heavenly Riddle

Most Christians have some awareness of the snake image in John and how that comes from the Old Testament. Many are also aware of the Old Testament background to the phrase *the Son of Man*.

The third aspect of the words of Y'shua to Nicodemus is the least understood. This concerns the riddle of heavenly ascending and descending. Here are Jesus' words again:

> No one has ever gone into heaven except the one who came from heaven—the Son of Man (John 3:13).

It is important for us to remember that the Lord was speaking to an expert in the teachings of the Hebrew Bible. He was stretching his mind in very new ways in order to help him to come to faith, to stand in the light instead of the darkness.

## The Wisdom of Agur

These words from Y'shua take us to one of the least trodden paths of the Bible, the teaching of Agur in Proverbs 30. Agur is something of a mystery. We do not know who he was, when he lived, or where. We suspect that he was not even a Hebrew writer. Rather, like King Lemuel (Proverbs 31:1-9), Agur is an example of a non-Israelite wise man who came to know Yahweh and whose wisdom became a part of the international flavoring of the Hebrew Book of Proverbs.

His part of the book begins inauspiciously enough. He seems to boast in his ignorance:

> I am the most ignorant of men;
>> I do not have a man's understanding.
> I have not learned wisdom,
>> nor have I knowledge of the Holy One
>> (Proverbs 30:2-3).

Yet in verse 5 he speaks in conventional wisdom, and the rest of his little book forms an integral part of the book of Proverbs.

It is in verse 4 that we have the mystery . . . and the surprise:

> Who has gone up to heaven and come down?
>> Who has gathered up the wind in
>> the hollow of his hands?
> Who has wrapped up the waters in his cloak?
>> Who has established all the ends of the earth?

In this passage we have the words of Y'shua. Here is the tying together of water and wind, causing us to remember the words of our Lord to Nicodemus concerning the two births, the work of the Spirit and its comparison to the wind. Moreover, here is the question concerning ascending and descending from the heavens. The obvious answer to these questions is *Yahweh*.

This verse in Proverbs 30 concludes with these words:

> What is his name, and the name of his son?
>> Tell me if you know!

Think again of the words of Y'shua:

32

No one has ever gone into heaven except the one who came from heaven—the Son of Man who is in heaven (John 3:13).

To a learned teacher of the Jews, Jesus answered an age-old question hidden away in a lost pocket of wisdom literature. He answered the question by saying, "It is I!"

What is the name of the one who holds the wind in his fists, who binds the waters in a garment, who established the ends of the earth?

His name is Yahweh.

What is the name of his Son?

His name is Y'shua.
Jesus.
Son of Man.
Son of God.

In these ways our Savior made incontestably strong assertions of his deity. In these ways he showed how the Scriptures all point to him.

## Y'shua—the Heart of Scripture

Y'shua is the heart of the Scripture.
The Old Testament is preparation for him.
The New Testament epistles are explanations of him.

But the gospels have the central story of the Bible, for it is in the gospels that we learn the story of Y'shua.

For these reasons there is a practice in some liturgical churches to give special honor to the reading of the gospels. In these churches there will often be a stated reading from the Old Testament and then from the epistles. These two readings will be made with the congregation seated. Then, for the reading of the gospel lesson, the congregation will stand. The standing is not meant to say these readings are more inspired than the others, but rather that they are the centerpiece of our faith.

Is there any wonder, then, that Y'shua spoke to his disciples as he did that evening of the first Easter? He told them that all things written in the Hebrew Scriptures had to be fulfilled.

Now he stood before them with all things fulfilled.

How great their joy must have been!

And how deep our joy, as we read these words and enter into them anew with wonder and worship to the risen one!

# 3

## Y'shua and the Psalms

**O**nce again, let's go back to the scene where the risen Lord appears to his astonished disciples. Because these words of the Savior are so very important for us, let's read them again with care. Jesus said to them,

> This is what I told you while I was still with you: Everything must be fulfilled that is written about me in the Law of Moses, the Prophets and the Psalms (Luke 24:44).

Jesus then opened their minds so they were able to understand these Scriptures. He told them:

> This is what is written: The Messiah will suffer and rise from the dead on the third day, and repentance and forgiveness of sins will be preached in his name to all nations, beginning at Jerusalem. You are witnesses of these things (Luke 24:46-48).

### Paul's Gospel of Y'shua

Years later Paul the apostle was to say much the same thing as he explained the central meaning of the gospel message. Paul wrote to the church at Corinth to remind them of the very basic nature of the Christian faith and how central to that faith is the resurrection of the Lord Jesus Christ.

Many who have read Paul's words in 1 Corinthians 15:3-5 have assumed there are three essential elements to the gospel message:

(1)   that the Messiah died for our sins,
(2)   that he was buried, and
(3)   that he rose again on the third day.

Many sermons have been preached along these lines, especially on Easter Sunday mornings!

## Two Points

A close reading of the text with attention to structure, however, reveals that there are *two* elements to the gospel message, not three:

(1)   the Messiah died for our sins, and
(2)   he rose again on the third day.

The burial of Jesus is not the second element of the message, but a confirmation of his death. For both his death and his resurrection there were scriptural predictions and historical validations. Here is this well-known text written structurally to show these important features:

For what I received I passed on to you as of first importance:
(1)   that Christ died for our sins
      (a) according to the Scriptures,
      (b) that he was buried,
(2)   that he was raised on the third day
      (a) according to the Scriptures,
      (b) and that he appeared to Peter, and then
      to the Twelve
          (1 Corinthians 15:3-5).

When we read the text in this way we find there are two major elements to the gospel account, and each of these elements is buttressed by two factors:

(1)   it was written in the Scriptures, and
(2)   it was observed in history.

So now we may state with great confidence the fullness of the gospel message:

36

- The death of Y'shua was predicted by Scripture and was validated by his burial.
- The resurrection of Y'shua was predicted by Scripture and was validated by his appearances to many people after death.

The apostle says what the Savior said: The Scriptures of God attested to the gospel story long before the Savior was ever born. The two principal factors, his death and resurrection, should have been expected by the reader of the Hebrew Bible.

## According to the Scriptures

As we think back to the words of the resurrected Jesus to the disciples, we may note that he speaks of the entire Scriptures as attesting these things. When Jesus spoke of the Law of Moses, the Prophets, and the Psalms, he was speaking of the whole Bible. The Hebrew Bible is divided into precisely those three sections.

- The Law of Moses is a way of speaking of the first five books of the Bible, Genesis through Deuteronomy.
- The Prophets include what we think of as the books of the prophets (except for Daniel), plus the early books of history (Joshua, Judges, Samuel, and Kings).
- The Psalms head the last section of the Bible, sometimes called the Writings, which includes the books of poetry and wisdom, the stories of Ruth and Esther, plus the books of Daniel, Ezra-Nehemiah, and Chronicles.

Since Jesus says each of these three sections of the Bible points to his death and resurrection, we may assert some major concepts respecting the Savior and the Scriptures:

- All of the Scripture points to the Savior.
- Each part of the Hebrew Bible looks forward to him.

**The Book of Psalms**

In this book, we will focus on the book of Psalms and see some of the ways in which it points to the Savior. We will learn that the psalms speak amazingly fully of the Savior, pointing to his incarnation, life, death, resurrection, and coming kingdom.

This book is not an exhaustive study of the psalms and the Savior. We will look at only a few quotations of the psalms in the New Testament. To study them all would require a considerably larger work than this. There are approximately 360 quotations from the Hebrew Bible in the New Testament. Nearly one third (112) of these are from Psalms. This is remarkable. The New Testament is awash with the psalms of Israel!

Y'shua is Lord of song!

I have always been impressed with the psalms in the life of the Savior. They speak of Y'shua's entire life; but *the psalms are particularly the libretto of his passion and his triumph over death*. The psalms, in short, present the New Testament gospel of the Lord Jesus Christ.

As we grow in our realization that the psalms are music and they present the words for the gospel of the Savior, it becomes more and more apparent that *the true singer of the psalms is Jesus*.

**In His Life and in His Death**

Jesus sang the psalms of Israel throughout his life. When he came to Jerusalem with his parents for the Feast of the Passover, he sang the Songs of Ascent (Psalms 120-134) with his family. Further, in celebrating the Passover feast each year he would sing the Hallel psalms (Psalms 113-118, 136), as would all Jewish families who kept the festival rightly.

It was particularly during passion week that the psalms came alive in his mouth. As we shall see, Psalm 118 marked his entrance into the city as the one who has come in the name of Yahweh (verse 26). Psalm 116 presented him with the words for lifting the cup of salvation (verse 13) and anticipating his death (verse 15). Psalm 22 gave him the words to utter his grief on the cross (verses 1-21), and the words of Psalm 31:5 were his last on the cross, "Into your hands I commit my spirit" (see Luke 23:46).

The psalms gave the Savior words to express his expectation of life after death as well. We usually think of Psalm 16:8-11 in this regard (see the apostolic preaching of Peter in Acts 2:25-28, 31). In addition, we may point to Psalm 22:22-26 as the confident words of the Savior to express his hope of resurrection, and to verses 27-31 of his trust in the future preaching of the gospel to the ends of the earth.

*Jesus is Lord of Song!*

The psalms are his songs. They are not only about him, they belong to him. And he sang them as the sweetest singer of all.

The great biblical scholar Saint Augustine was so taken with the role of the psalms in the New Testament story of our Lord Jesus Christ that he termed Jesus *iste cantator psalmorum*, "He, the singer of the psalms."

## The Singer

Now we do not mean to say that Jesus was the first singer of the psalms. We do not even say that the psalms began as the songs of Jesus. The psalms were the music of Israel. The psalms were the songs of the people of God in a time that began long before the birth of the Savior.

Yet the Spirit of God so worked in the writers of these varied songs, that while they expressed in them their own words of praise to God ("God is good!") and their own words of lament before God ("Life is tough!"), their songs became in fact Jesus' songs.

Some writers speak of the arbitrary way in which the New Testament writers use the psalms to speak of Jesus. In the study that follows, we will show things that are not arbitrary at all, but providential—and wonderful!

In this study we will follow the interpretation of the psalms given by Jesus himself to his astonished disciples. It was he who said that the Scriptures speak of his suffering and death and of his resurrection and the preaching of his gospel. It was he who said that these things were written in the Law of Moses and the Prophets. It was he who said that these are written as well in the Psalms.

Come now, as we open the hymnal of Israel. We will hear words of David and Asaph, of the guild of Korah and of unknown poets.

Preeminently we will hear the words of the Savior.

*Y'shua is Lord of Song!*

# PART TWO

# Y'shua
# The Singer
# of the
# Psalms

CHAPTER
# 4

## Body
## Song

**J**esus opened things both ways. He opened the Scriptures to his disciples, and he opened their hearts to the Scriptures.

I wonder where he began? I wonder what texts he used?

### Once in a Garden

When the Savior turned to the Law of Moses, did he go all the way back to the text we now call the "first gospel"? Perhaps he did. Perhaps he pointed to the cryptic words of Genesis 3:15 and found in them mention of himself, his struggle against and final victory over the evil one.

The scene was the Garden of Eden. It was evening; the man and the woman had just thrown Paradise away. Our first parents were huddling in shame. The snake hissed with supercilious disdain, believing his victory to be complete.

Then Yahweh spoke. He spoke to the serpent who had been the occasion for the fall of man:

> And I will put enmity
>     between you and the woman,
>     and between your offspring and hers;
> he will crush your head,
>     and you will strike his heel (Genesis 3:15).

Isn't this passage so like God's mercy? In the context of judgment on our first parents because of their rebellion in the Garden, he brings judgment as well on their nemesis. But in judgment he gives the first words of his grace, the promise of the Savior. And he said these words to the

43

snake! As we overhear them, we are drawn into the most profound mystery of time: God will work through the seed of the woman to bring ultimate judgment upon the seed of the serpent.

I wonder. Did Jesus direct the thoughts of his disciples all the way back to this event that happened once in a garden?

## Once on a Hilltop

Perhaps the Savior pointed out the remarkable story of the near sacrifice of Isaac, where father Abraham met his ultimate test of faithfulness to Yahweh. You may remember that it was at the hill of Moriah that an aged man held his ritual sacrificial knife against the neck of his beloved son. Just beneath the skin was the carotid artery. The pressure was firm, but the old man's heart was breaking.

This was the son of promise, his uniquely begotten son. This was Isaac whom he loved. And there he stood, a father contemplating the death of his son. It was an unspeakable moment, an unbearable reality.

Just before the knife plunged into its unnatural home, a voice shouted from heaven, stifling the sobs of the father. The voice called his name. Twice. The voice told him to stop his hand. Twice. The voice heaped blessing upon the father for his willingness to journey on the path into God-forsakenness and to continue to believe in the promises of Yahweh. Those promises were in his son. And his son would live!

Abraham's faith had been so profound in the belief Yahweh would fulfill his promise in his beloved son Isaac, Abraham dared to believe that if his son were to be put to death, somehow God would have to bring him back to life.

As Abraham and his son left the servants for their walk together toward cruel death, Abraham calmed the servants with the words that he and the lad were going to worship God together. And then he said, "Together we will return." The Hebrew verb in Genesis 22:5 is a strong form of deliberate determination. The words at the end of the verse may be translated, "and then we are determined to come back to you."

The writer of the book of Hebrews picked up on that

strong verbal form and found in it the exquisite depths of the faith of Abraham. Hebrews says, "Abraham reasoned that God could raise the dead, and figuratively speaking, he did receive Isaac back from death" (Hebrews 11:19).

One day, on a spot not very far from where Abraham's son was spared, there was another son who was not spared. On that latter occasion there was to be no voice. No last minute reprieve. No animal caught in the thicket nearby. Nothing to stop the pain of death. Nothing to assuage the grieving heart of that father.

Did Jesus explain to his disciples what his death and the near death of Isaac had in common? How the binding of Isaac points to the nailing of the arms and feet of the Savior? How the heart of Abraham pictures the heart of God? How the compliance of Isaac foreshadows the compliance of Y'shua?

Did Jesus take his disciples back to this text that speaks of the model of faith enacted once upon a hilltop?

**Once in the Darkness**

As we move from the Law of Moses to the Prophets, we wonder again what texts he might have selected, what he might have said. Perhaps Jesus directed his disciples to the prophetic words concerning the promises of the birth of the Savior. One of those passages is the celebrated text of Isaiah 9.

That passage has its context in a period of deep gloom and joylessness for the people of Judah and Jerusalem. The Assyrian army had invaded the Levant in three successive campaigns under their leader Tiglath Pileser III.

In 734 B.C. they campaigned down the Via Maris, the way of the sea. They made all of the coastlands their own, all the way to the brook of Egypt.

In 733 B.C. the Assyrians trampled through Israel, making the northern kingdom of the Hebrew peoples an Assyrian province. Only the capital city of Samaria was spared destruction, and it had only a decade left to live.

In 732 B.C. the armies came back west once more. In this campaign they took possession of the region of Syria and trans-Jordan.

In these three successive campaigns the armies of Assyria established utter supremacy in the northern Hebrew lands. And down south, in Judah and Jerusalem, there was the gray pallor of a funeral parlor. Who knows but Judah may be next, that the south might be trampled like the north?

In this context of fear and gloom the prophet Isaiah was given one of the most wonderful promises of all. To a people who were living in the darkness of fear and in the gloom of despair, there was coming light and joy!

- *Light was coming*! Light that would burst upon a people who felt condemned forever to darkness.
- *Joy was coming*! Joy to a people who must have felt that they would never smile again!

Light in the darkness.
Joy in the gloom.
How should such things be? Because one day there would be the birth of a baby!

> For to us a child is born,
>     to us a son is given,
>     and the government will be on his shoulders,
> And he will be called
>     Wonderful Counselor, Mighty God,
>     Everlasting Father, Prince of Peace (Isaiah
>     9:6).

How like God! How like his grace! How like his unexpectedness! Darkness and gloom will both be transformed. Light and joy are coming; they will come in the birth of a child!

Did Jesus open this text to the ears and hearts of his disciples? Did they see in these words what we see in them today? Did they understand that it was he who had come as light and joy? It was he who came in his humanity as the child who was born. It was he who came in his deity as the son who was given.

There he stood before them now, not as a little baby, but as the adult man they had come to know and to love.

There he stood before them as the one whose death had destroyed their joy and robed them altogether in darkness.

There he stood, *fully alive.*

And they looked on him.

- Joy came that night.
- Light came that night.

## Once in a Manger

I wonder what other texts in the Prophets Jesus might have opened to them that night. Surely he must have directed his disciples to think of the words of Micah which also spoke of the promise of his birth.

You remember this verse. We think of it every Christmas. It may be the only verse of Micah that many Christians have ever read. The book as a whole is grander than this verse, but had Micah said only these words, we would bless him forever:

> But you, Bethlehem Ephrathah,
>     though you are small among the clans of Judah,
> out of you will come for me
>     one who will be ruler over Israel,
> whose origins are from of old,
>     from ancient times (Micah 5:2).

These words of the prophet Micah mesh well with the words of Isaiah, his contemporary. The promise is made in a context of pain and despair, a time of assault against the ruler of Israel and siege against its people (Micah 5:1).

But one day *he* would come. One day he who has been from ages past would enter human drama as man. One day he who is ruler of eternity would become a human king. One day he who has been in the bosom of the Father forever would come to earth to express more fully than ever before was possible the nature and heart and wonder of God.

And when he comes, what wonder that will be! Micah puts it this way:

He will stand and shepherd his flock
  in the strength of the LORD,
  in the majesty of the name of the LORD his
God.
And they will live securely, for then his greatness
  will reach to the ends of the earth.
And he will be their peace (Micah 5:4-5a).

When he comes it will be as shepherd. But no ordinary shepherd will he be. He will have the power of God and the authority of Yahweh to shepherd his people. His presence will bring lasting security and universal dominion. And he himself will be *shalom*, peace—everything right and as it ought to be! He is Prince of Peace. He *is* Shalom.

And there he stands before his disciples! In his person are the fulfillments of these words. There he is! *Our* peace. Our Shalom. To them, his first words were words of peace. Was it this text in Micah, moving from the manger in Bethlehem to the rule of Christ's glory, that he opened to his disciples that night?

**Once in Heaven**

And the psalms. What psalm might he have opened? What psalm might have tied together all these texts from the Law of Moses and the Prophets?

Perhaps it was the words of Psalm 40:6-8. Here is a song sung even in heaven.

The fortieth psalm is an impassioned song of God's deliverance. It is a poem that reflects upon the hand of God reaching down in the past to deliver a hurting man. It is a poem that also speaks of hope for deliverance in the present. It is a poem that looks forward to renewed praise of God in the community of the future.

Psalm 40 is all of these things. And it is considerably more. It begins as a poem of David. It becomes the song of the eternal Son of God in heaven above before he entered human history. This psalm is the libretto of the incarnation. Here we have the words that Jesus sang before becoming born of blessed Mary. This psalm is consummate mystery.

The psalm speaks of the life of the Savior as well. Micah

said in his prophecy that this Jesus, born in Bethlehem, was the eternal one whose goings forth have been forever. Yet in becoming man, the eternal one became weak. When he became man, the almighty one became needy. As man there was a sense in which he was as dependent upon the Father as is any woman or man of faith. Hence, the last words of this poem speak of the prayer life of the Savior:

> Yet I am poor and needy;
>> may the Lord think of me.
> You are my help and my deliverer;
>> O my God, do not delay (Psalm 40:17).

In such words we have the model of prayer in the Savior. Truly no one ever prayed like Jesus. And in no one was prayer more mysterious than in him.

In his life the Savior was resolutely dependent upon the strength of his father in heaven, a model to all weaker women and men who tend so often to act as though they do not need this absolute dependence on God in their walk and life.

An early verse in the psalm gives a beatitude on resolute fidelity to Yahweh, a beatitude which came to pass daily in the life of Jesus:

> Blessed is the man
>> who makes the LORD his trust,
> who does not look to the proud,
>> to those who turn aside to false gods (Psalm 40:4).

## Heaven's Song

We will return to the beginning of this psalm in a later chapter. For the present, let us see the words that are the song of Jesus in heaven just before he became wrapped in the small dimensions of humanity.

> Sacrifice and offering you did not desire,
>> but my ears you have pierced;
> burnt offerings and sin offerings
>> you did not require.

Then I said, "Here I am, I have come—
  it is written about me in the scroll.
I desire to do your will, O my God;
  your law is within my heart" (Psalm 40:6-8).

This passage is so impressive in so many ways, one scarcely knows where to begin in approaching its message. There are two outstanding elements, however, on which we must dwell briefly.

## Not Sacrifice Alone

First, we find in these words the genuine insight that all readers of the Bible need to have respecting the inner essence of Torah. The desire of Yahweh was never just for rivers of blood splashing against his altars. God is not ghoulish. His desire and intent were always for righteousness in the inner man.

The sacrificial system was not given to Israel as a means of reaching salvation. The system was God's gracious provision to a saved community for the people to maintain ritual purity before him.

Have you ever started to read the Bible through in one year? Do you remember your exhilaration when you began? Genesis went well for you, I suspect. The "begats" interrupt the narrative only on occasion. The rest of the book ripples with human interest. From the story of Abraham to the story of Joseph, Genesis is a delight.

Exodus begins well also. There is the epic story of the deliverance of Israel from Egypt under the leadership of one of the greatest figures in all of human history—Moses, God's servant. The latter part of Exodus slows down, with much attention given to laws and ritual; but anyone can continue to the end of a book that begins with such drama.

Then comes Leviticus. And then concludes the reading of the Scripture!

We can hardly get into Leviticus. It seems so devoid of human interest. It is filled with much that seems so foreign to us, so dusty with the past. If it were just dusty with lint, perhaps we might persevere. But it is dusty with dried blood. The book talks incessantly about sacrificial ritual, and we feel so far away . . . Why not turn from it?

But the point of Leviticus to the people who first received it was not how awful it was that God demanded so much of them. Leviticus was not a stone wall which they had to climb over, dig under, walk around, or just hit their heads against.

Leviticus was a pathway for them. A pathway for life. To a community that had a relationship with Yahweh based on his mercy, his grace, his power, his election, his work—the book of Leviticus came along to keep that relationship open and free.

The proper approach to Leviticus is not to say, "How could the people stand it?" but rather, "Oh, the mercy of God, who, maintaining his holiness, has made the way clear for sinful people to approach him!"

The inner issue was always righteousness of the inner man, never the bare actions of ritual sacrifice.

## Basic Issues

This was taught already by Moses in Torah. One of the finest explanations is given in Moses' last work, the homily of Deuteronomy. The most important question a man or woman might ask of God is answered in this place:

> And now, O Israel, what does the LORD your God ask of you but to fear the LORD your God, to walk in all his ways, to love him, to serve the LORD your God with all your heart and with all your soul, and to observe the LORD's commands and decrees that I am giving you today for your own good? (Deuteronomy 10:12-13).

These verses link seemingly contradictory responses to God: fear and love, God's commands and the people's good. But these are not contradictory. They all work together. God's commands for his people were intended for good, not for their hurt. God's desire for his people was a reverent fear and a loving devotion. Singleness of purpose, focus on him only, total devotion to Yahweh—these are the genuine issues of biblical faith.

Sacrifice was a means. It was never the end. Sacrifice

51

kept the access open to God; it was never to be a barricade to his mercy. Sacrifice of animals pointed forward to the death of the Savior; the killing of goats and sheep never satisfied God's demands.

The prophets knew this, for they too had read Torah. Hear the words of Micah. He asks the rhetorical question,

> With what shall I come before the LORD
> and bow down before the exalted God?
> (Micah 6:6).

Micah presents the provisional answer that God's desire is (just) the sacrificial animal on the bloodied altar. Hence, he asks what sort of burnt offerings will finally please Yahweh. Must one bring burnt offerings of young calves? How many? Should God desire rams, must they be in the thousands? If he commands the offerings of olive oil, should they be in ten thousand rivers? And if it is really sacrifice that God desires, must I finally bring my firstborn son to appease him?

No! Such was not the true teaching of Torah. Micah points back to the true intention of God:

> He has showed you, O man, what is good.
> And what does the LORD require of you?
> To act justly and to love mercy
> and to walk humbly with your God (Micah
> 6:8).

These words take us back to Psalm 40. Torah, Prophets, and Psalms agree: It is not sacrifice alone, but true works of righteousness from the inner man that God desires. The poet says:

> Sacrifice and offering you did not desire,
> but my ears you have pierced;
> burnt offerings and sin offerings
> you did not require.
> Then I said, "Here I am, I have come—
> it is written about me in the scroll.
> I desire to do your will, O my God;
> your law is within my heart" (Psalm 40:6-8).

## Here I Am

The second major element we must observe in Psalm 40:6-8 is the way in which this text is the song of Y'shua. We know this is the case because of the quotation of these verses by Hebrews 10:5-7. This quotation is remarkably dramatic; the New Testament writer says that these words from a song of David were sung in heaven.

As is often the case, the New Testament writer has quoted not from the Hebrew original, but from the Greek translation of the Old Testament that we call the Septuagint. For the most part, the wording is very similar to the verses we have quoted from the psalm. One significant change is made, however. Where the psalmist speaks of God digging out the cavity of his ear, the New Testament writer says, "but a body you prepared for me" (Hebrews 10:5).

The expression "my ears you have pierced" has been thought by some to refer to the mark of a voluntary slave whose ear is pierced as a mark of his willingness to obey the word of his master (Exodus 21:6; Deuteronomy 15:17). This would certainly fit the context of inward response to God as a voluntary servant. It flows well with the words of the inward desire to do the will of God because the law of God is within one's heart.

But I believe it more likely that the Hebrew word *kārâ* in Psalm 40:6 means not to pierce the lobe of the ear, but to bore the cavity of the ear. That is, this is a highly poetic image of God's fashioning the ear of the believer as a receiving orifice of the commands of God.

In these words, then, David asserts his readiness and willingness to be the true servant of Yahweh. He has come to do the pleasure of God. He steps forward with boldness and majesty.

## A Body!

These are more than the words of David. They are preeminently the words of the Savior in heaven just before he came to take on the flesh of humanity which the Father had prepared for him.

The image of digging out the ears is a part for the whole. God has done more than work out the intricacies of the human ear. He has made the whole body, of which the ear is just a part.

God has prepared a *body* for the Lord Jesus. The ears are just a part of that whole body.

This use of language is similar to that of Isaiah when he stood before the majesty of Yahweh. He was stunned with the holiness of God and was reminded of his own unworthiness. Isaiah cried out that he was a man of unclean lips (Isaiah 6:5). This was not because he had a blemish on his lips! In the context of praising God in the royal scene above, Isaiah realized he could not join in that praise. His lips—a part for the whole—were unclean. When the live coal touched the lips of Isaiah (verse 7), he received a thorough forgiveness, not just a spot cleaning.

Hence, the writer to the Hebrews is able to develop the theology of Psalm 40:6-8 and to relate it explicitly to the Lord Jesus. In fact, it is the New Testament writer who says that these words were the very words of the Messiah before he came into the world.

The writer speaks of the inability of animal sacrifices in Old Testament days to make people perfect. He says, "But those sacrifices are an annual reminder of sins, because it is impossible for the blood of bulls and goats to take away sins" (Hebrews 10:3-4). Then the writer says these stunning words:

Therefore, when Christ came into the world, he said:

"Sacrifice and offering you did not desire,
   but a body you prepared for me;
with burnt offerings and sin offerings
   you were not pleased.
Then I said, 'Here I am—it is written about me in
the scroll—
   I have come to do your will, O God'" (Hebrews
   10:5- 7).

**And Still He Has a Body**

What a Savior he is! Can you imagine him standing before the disciples in his resurrection body, gesturing with his arms at the flesh that God had prepared for him? The body of the Lord Jesus was now glorified; but it was still a body.

We simply do not understand what it means for the eternal one, whose goings have been from everlasting, to have taken upon himself a body for all eternity.

All we really know is that when the time was right, he said to his Father the words of this psalm:

> Here I am, I have come—
> it is written about me in the scroll.
> To do your will, O my God, is my desire;
> your law is within my heart (Psalm 40:7-8).

And then he stood before his disciples and opened things both ways. He opened the Scriptures to them. He opened them to the Scriptures.

So he does for us.

# 5

# Teacher's Song

*Overheard in a fast food booth:*

"I don't know much about the Bible. You know? I mean, like, some things are a little wild and spooky. You know, like the prophecy scene. And, like, I saw *The Omen*. You know? And, like, that about weirded me out."

"I know what you mean. Like in *Ghostbusters*. Remember the line: 'This is real Old Testament stuff'?"

"Oh, yeah! That's what I mean! Well, anyway, about Jesus. Well, you know, he's supposed to be God and all. But I'm not really into the Jesus trip. I guess the one thing I really know is that Jesus was a really good teacher. You know?"

"Right. Right on. I mean, that's heavy."

"Right. Mega-heavy! I mean, Jesus really had it all together, you know? I mean, Jesus may not have been God and all, but he was really cool."

"Excellent! He was kind, too. Not like that Old Testament stuff. Jesus doesn't slime. Remember in *Ghostbusters*?"

"I'd like to forget; you know? Hey, man. Is that the 'new' Coke ®?"

## Jesus the Teacher

Jesus *is* the great teacher. But he was not always what one might expect in a great teacher.

We tend to link a great teacher with a great institution. Jesus had no such ties.

We tend to think of a great teacher as one who makes difficult things less complex. Jesus seemed to show new complexities even in simple things.

We tend to anticipate that a great teacher helps us face life more independently. Jesus kept insisting that life must be lived in full dependence on another.

We tend to associate a great teacher with technical language of his or her field. Jesus used simple language and everyday things.

We tend to link a great teacher to his or her brilliant, erudite students. Those who learned best from Jesus were the poor, the lonely, the simple.

We tend to think of a great teacher in the setting of a classroom. Jesus' classroom was a hillside overlooking the Sea of Galilee, a corner of a living room, a walk along a path, a small space in a little boat.

Today we tend to look for a teacher to use multi-media tools. Jesus' tools were the heavens, the fields, mountains and birds, storms and sheep, a vineyard, a well, and a banquet. In short, whatever was around he would use as a teaching tool.

But teacher he was. One of the common designations given to our Lord by his contemporaries was the Hebrew word *rabbi*. This was the way that Nicodemus spoke to him (John 3:2). The word *rabbi* refers to an authoritative teacher, worthy of respect, learned and honorable—a *master* (see Matthew 23:1-7).

It was a very high compliment for his teaching skills that Y'shua was called "rabbi" by learned men. But Jesus did not always accept the title "rabbi," because he was well aware of the thoughts of the men who might attempt to use that term to gain his confidence. Ever knowing, the Lord knew what was in the heart of man. He responded accordingly.

As in the case of the ancient Pharisees, some moderns speak of Jesus as a good teacher, but deny all claims he made concerning himself and avoid all demands he might make in their lives. By saying, "Ah yes, Jesus; a great teacher!" some people really hope to avoid him altogether.

Some true Christians, in reaction, are fearful of speaking of Jesus as a teacher at all. They are afraid of being linked with the crowd who evade him by faint praise.

But teacher he was. Rabbi—*master*—he was. Jesus *the Wise* is a phrase we must learn to appreciate.

By his death and resurrection, the Lord Jesus brought about our salvation. But the death and resurrection of Y'shua have meaning in his teaching. He anticipated his death, he endured the suffering and shame, and he authenticated his person in his triumph. All of these things he did within the context of genuine teaching ministry.

## A Good Teacher

Finally, let's set it to rest once more. The teaching of Jesus is great only if the content of his teaching conforms to reality. A creative teacher who teaches falsehood is not a great teacher. A poor teacher who deals inadequately with truth is not made great just because she or he tries to confront great issues. But a great teacher who brings pure perspectives on reality—ah, there is the seedbed for real teaching! There is the teaching of Y'shua!

If Jesus were not who he claimed to be, then he was not a good teacher. He would have been a charlatan and a deceiver. In Israel a false teacher, like a false prophet, was to be condemned, not indulged.

At the same time, if we really believe Jesus to have been a great teacher, why don't we spend more time listening to his words, thinking along the new pathways of his leading, and heeding his instruction?

## Offices of the Christ

In classical Protestant theology we have been encouraged to think of Jesus Christ as having three principal offices. These are Prophet, Priest, and King. That is, as Prophet, Jesus is superior to Moses. As Priest, he is grander than Aaron. As King, he is more excellent than David.

It is time to add to our understanding of the offices of Christ. There is a neglected office of Christ. He *is also Teacher*. Y'shua is the Wise whose wisdom surpasses Solomon. Jesus is the Sage whose wisdom was anticipated by the imagery of Lady Wisdom in Proverbs 1-9. Jesus is the great Rabbi, the master teacher of the ages, who came to explain very God: "No one has ever seen God, but God the only Son, who is at the Father's side, has made him known" (John 1:18). The apostle Paul affirms that in Christ "are hidden all the treasures of wisdom and knowledge" (Colossians 2:3). *Jesus is Wisdom.*

## From His Youth

Jesus was Wisdom from his youth. The narrative of Luke describes how the the precocious boy Jesus came with his family to Jerusalem at the Feast of the Passover in his twelfth year (Luke 2:41-50). After the feast, his parents began on their way back to Nazareth. They discovered he was not with them! They panicked when they could not find him. They rushed back to the city and searched for him three days. Finally they found him sitting in the courts of the temple interacting with the learned teachers of Torah, answering and questioning them with a skill that amazed them all. Why the learned teachers of Torah had not shown some concern for the stress of the parents of this bright boy is not given. The Bible does record the subsequent, very human interplay between the parents and the boy. But then Luke notes the ongoing obedience of the young Jesus, likely something that Mary told the gospel writer (Luke 2:48-51).

His maturation is summarized in these words: "And Jesus grew in wisdom and stature, and in favor with God and men" (Luke 2:52). These words fulfill the wisdom ideal:

> Then you will win favor and a good name
>     in the sight of God and man (Proverbs 3:4).

Jesus is the Wise.

## How He Taught

When we think of the ethical teaching of Jesus we usually think of the Sermon on the Mount (Matthew 5-7). Those who heard him were astonished at this masterful presentation. Matthew comments, "When Jesus had finished saying these things, the crowds were amazed at his teaching, because he taught as one who had authority, and not as their teachers of the law" (Matthew 7:28-29).

His teaching was revolutionary, distinct from what the people were used to hearing. His teaching was compelling, bearing the inner witness of the impress of the Spirit of God. His teaching was innovative, presenting the truth of God to the crowds and not just to the intellectual elite.

*But his teaching was not new.*

The most impressive element of the teaching of Jesus is that it is the full outgrowth of the central teaching of Scripture. After all, this is his own assertion:

> Do not think that I have come to abolish the Law or the Prophets; I have not come to abolish them but to fulfill them. I tell you the truth, until heaven and earth disappear, not the smallest letter, not the least stroke of a pen, will by any means disappear from the Law until everything is accomplished" (Matthew 5:17-18).

## As a Rose

Think of the Bible as a rose.

- The Law of Moses is the rose in the fullness of the bud stage. The whole flower is there, but it is not yet opened.
- The Prophets and the Writings show the rose beginning to open, exposing more fully the color, fragrance, and beauty of the flower.
- In the Gospel teaching of Jesus, the flower is now quite open, boasting fully the beauty of the flower that was always there.
- In the Epistles, the flower is full blown, showing by the extension and separation of individual petals more detail and pattern than could have been seen before that time.

Too often we look at the individual petals and think of one of them as fully defining the rose. In fact, by looking too closely at one petal we may lose perspective on the flower. Or we may look at one petal (an epistle text) and think that this is new truth, never before known.

61

Yet the petal is but a part of the flower and needs to be seen in the context of the fullness of the flower. The petal was always a part of the flower. It is only in the later stages of the opening of the rose that we may see some of the fine detail. But the petal was always there.

All that Jesus taught on the ethical plane was already a part of the flower of Scripture. The flower was beginning to open in the prophets and the wisdom writings. But it is in the teaching of Y'shua that the flower is fully open.

Jesus did not substitute blooms. He did not practice spiritual sleight of hand. The flower of the Scripture is the same flower that has been opening since the time of Moses.

Too often Christians think that in Jesus all truth is new. The real point of the teaching ministry of Y'shua is that in him truth is made clear. He reveals and explains. His teaching displays the beauty of the flower that was God's gift at the beginning.

**In Parables**

Matthew 13 presents one of the most intriguing developments in the teaching ministry of Y'shua. The chapter begins with the Teacher so pressed by the crowd who had come to hear him that he had to move from the shore to a boat to keep from being pushed into the water by the anxious crowd.

Jesus taught that day in parables. He told a story that has been retold innumerable times, the parable of the sower (Matthew 13:3-8). At the end of his story, Jesus said these mysterious words: "He who has ears, let him hear" (verse 9).

The disciples were puzzled. They asked him why he had spoken in parables. His response was to quote from the Scriptures to show that it has always been the manner of God to present truth accessibly to the true seeker for God, but to make even the accessibility of truth an impossibility for the insincere.

God's word is a gift. He gives to whom he wills as he wills. Jesus said,

The knowledge of the secrets of the kingdom of heaven has been given to you, but not to them. Whoever has will be given more, and he will have an abundance. Whoever does not have, even what he has will be taken from him. This is why I speak to them in parables:

Though seeing, they do not see;
   though hearing, they do not hear or understand
(Matthew 13:11-13).

The use of parable in the teaching of Y'shua was in fulfillment of a double prophecy: one from the Prophets and one from the Psalms. One was a prophecy of the obscuring of truth from unrepentant, evil men. The other was a prophecy of the revealing of truth to genuine and sincere people. Through the story form, Jesus was able to present his teaching to the righteous and to the wicked. In each hearer there were responses proceeding from his or her own inner nature. For some the teaching of Jesus was liberating and freeing—life itself. For others the teaching of Jesus was dulling and damning—the seed of death.

**As Isaiah**

Matthew presents first the model of Isaiah, which tells how the teaching of Jesus could condemn. Isaiah was commissioned by God to proclaim a message that would damn his hearers because of their increasing insensitivity to the truth of God (Isaiah 6:9- 10). These words are quoted by Matthew and are applied to the teaching of Jesus. The more that the wicked heard, the less they understood. The more that Jesus would teach, the less would they learn.

But to the righteous these words were life. Jesus said,

But blessed are your eyes because they see, and your ears because they hear. For I tell you the truth, many prophets and righteous men longed to see what you see but did not see it, and to hear what you hear but did not hear it (Matthew 13:16-17).

All of this was part of a plan. All was according to purpose. For the teaching of Jesus was based not only on the negative model of the judgmental ministry of Isaiah. It was also based on the *song of the teacher* in Psalm 78. This is the second aspect of prophetic fulfillment in the teaching of Jesus. In this case, the prophet is a hymnist, the prophecy a song:

> Jesus spoke all these things to the crowd in parables; he did not say anything to them without using a parable. So was fulfilled what was spoken through the prophet:

> "I will open my mouth in parables,
>   I will utter things hidden since the creation
>     of the world" (Matthew 13:34-35, quoting
>     Psalm 78:2).

The parabolic teaching of Jesus thus follows two prophetic models. By his stories he both obscured and revealed the truth of God. For one who has the ears to hear, his words are life itself. For one who has no ear for truth, his words are death.

Let's look a bit at the psalm that provides the hymnic-prophetic base for the teaching ministry of Jesus. This is the contemplative poem (Hebrew, *maskîl*) of Asaph, Psalm 78. In this psalm there are basic keys for interpreting and understanding the flow of Scripture from the Torah of Moses to the teaching of Y'shua.

The psalm begins in this way:

> O my people, hear my teaching;
>   listen to the words of my mouth (Psalm 78:1).

How like Moses all this is! How well these words show the interconnectedness of Scripture. They pull us back to Moses, and they propel us forward to Jesus. Compare, for example, the opening words of the last song of Moses:

> Listen, O heavens, and I will speak;
>   hear, O earth, the words of my mouth.
> Let my teaching fall like rain
>   and my words descend like dew,

like showers on new grass,
    like abundant rain on tender plants
        (Deuteronomy 32:1-2).

The words of Psalm 78 link Moses to Jesus, and they do it in song, for both sang the word of God. The words "my teaching" and "the words of my mouth" are words of Moses and the wisdom school. "My teaching" is literally "my Torah"—this points to Moses. "The words of my mouth" is a phrase that characterizes both the prophets and the wise. These are Old Testament values that Jesus embraces in his own teaching.

The verbs in the verse are built upon the noun "ears." The verb "hear" is literally "use your ears!" The verb "listen" is literally "extend your ear!" These subtleties of language are reflected by Jesus as he says, If you have ears, use them! This first verse is a strong command to work at listening to the teaching/Torah of the singer. The Savior is the new singer of this song.

**As Jesus**

Now comes the central declaration, the first part of which Matthew quotes:

I will open my mouth in parables,
    I will utter things hidden from of old—
things we have heard and known,
    things our fathers have told us
        (Psalm 78:2-3).

The Hebrew word translated "parable" is *māshāl*. This term has three aspects, each of which is fitting in this psalm and remarkably so in the teaching of Jesus. The three aspects of *māshāl* are: (1) proverb, (2) parable, and (3) oracle. Let's look at each of these.

**Proverb**

The wise of many cultures throughout world history used the *proverb* as a teaching device. It is especially prominent in the wisdom tradition in Israel. A proverb is characterized by three elements: (1) compactness, (2) memorability, and (3) transferability.

An example from our own tradition is the proverb, "A stitch in time saves nine." The three elements of a proverb are found here. It is compact: Six words express what a paragraph might describe. It is memorable: Rhythm and assonance help us to remember it. It is transferable: The proverb has to do with more than sewing up an unraveling thread; it may apply to many aspects of life.

Proverbs play a major role in the teaching of Jesus. We have already seen one of them in Matthew 13:13. Just before the quotation of the prophetic text from Isaiah, our Lord presents the proverb:

> Though seeing, they do not see;
>> though hearing, they do not hear or understand.

## Parable

The Hebrew word *māshāl* also means "parable." This use of the word emphasizes transferability. It speaks of one thing being *like* that. It is a hiding/revealing technique. It demands thought, not passivity.

Some have said that the lecture method (which is most common in modern teaching) allows the material of a professor's notes to go into the notes of his students without having gone through the mind of either. Today we might expect a classroom to be filled with tape recorders on each student's desk with a playback unit at the professor's lectern. The people don't have to be there. Tomorrow we might imagine an electronic transfer of knowledge from one mainframe computer to a personal computer at home. No one needs to listen.

The parable method demands thought. It is learning in process. The story pulls one in and then drags one out. The parable makes one think and to ask.

Those who had ears turned to Jesus to ask what he meant by his stories. To them he revealed the meaning. He still reveals himself today.

## Oracle

The third use of *māshāl* is of a prophetic oracle. In fact, one prominent use of this word in that sense is in the prophetic oracles of the improbable prophet Balaam (Numbers 23-24). Each of the seven oracles of Balaam is called a *māshāl* in Hebrew (see, for example, Numbers 23:7).

Certainly the Song of Moses in Deuteronomy 32 is also a *māshāl*—a prophetic oracle. The prophetic aspect has its authority in God.

The teaching of Jesus is regularly characterized by all three aspects of the Hebrew *māshāl*. In his teaching there is:

- *the proverb*, a witty insight on life, wry and memorable,
- *the parable*, a story told for its own sake for enjoyment and for teaching valuable lessons,
- *the oracle*, a use of prophetic diction, an authoritative declaration that may bring condemnation, confrontation, or consolation.

## Wisdom Model

So again we assert Jesus is the Wise. His teaching fulfills the model of wisdom in the Hebrew Bible, which in turn reaches back to the Law of Moses. The flower unfolds.

Wisdom is for all, not just for the elite. The psalmist speaks in grace to "my people" (Psalm 78:1). It is particularly the people of God to whom wisdom presents herself (Proverbs 1:20-21) and extends considerable mercies (Proverbs 3:1-3).

The center of wisdom in the Bible is the notion of the fear of Yahweh (see Proverbs 1:7; 2:5; 3:7, etc.). Wisdom is built into the universe that God has created (Proverbs 3:19-20). These two factors lead to a biblical view of learning. The believer has a key to learning that includes not only the joy of discovery, but the anticipation of worshiping God in the things one learns. Love of learning is a divine gift; it also leads rightly to praise of God, who is the giver.

Wisdom makes us think of God, who is the only Wise. As we think of his works, we think of his wisdom:

- his wisdom in creation
- his wisdom in redemption
- his wisdom in sovereignty
- his wisdom in providence
- his wisdom in the consummation of the ages.

As we think of wisdom, we think of the wisdom of the Savior in the varied aspects of his teaching. He presented wisdom for the whole man and for all people. We see this in:

- his teaching of the disciples
- his teaching of women
- his teaching of the crowds
- his teaching of intellectuals
- his teaching of children.

## Hidden Things

Psalm 78:2 presents both the parabolic teaching of the Lord and the disclosing teaching of Jesus: "I will utter things hidden from of old." The verb "utter" is literally the word "to bubble over." As he is so filled with wisdom, he opens his mouth and bubbles over with truth.

He reveals the hidden things. The "hidden things" are the riddles of life, the enigmas of existence, the secret things of God. These are hidden from of old, but they may be known even as they have been known by our fathers. They are a part of the flower.

The early verses of Psalm 78 emphasize how teaching the hidden things of God continues through time. Wisdom presents itself as new, yet it is old. Jesus presents his message as new, yet it is old. It is the continual unfolding of that which has already been. These are things which wise men and women have learned from their parents and which they pass on to their children (Psalm 78:3-4). This is the outgrowth of Deuteronomy 6:7, "Impress them on your children." The biblical wisdom tradition has its roots in Torah.

For each generation there must be a sense of the newness of learning; but the new is old. A major part of transgenerational teaching is to show how old truths relate to the new pressures of life. Similarly, the task of transcultural teaching is to show how old truths relate to new contexts.

The point of wisdom is not to hide, but to declare. Verse 4 begins, "We will not hide" these things. Wisdom does not obscure, but reveals; it does not destroy, but maintains.

And the emphasis is on children, the coming generation. Jesus, who has no child, is nonetheless in his wisdom the true parent of all who will listen.

This is the ultimate subject of wisdom:

> the praiseworthy deeds of the LORD,
>> his power, and the wonders he has done
>> (Psalm 78:4).

This curriculum leads to praising Yahweh for the glorious wonders he has done for his people.

The capstone is in verses 5-8. God's wonders include his word. He has spoken to his people and has commanded one generation to teach his wonders to the next so that the errors of the fathers would not be repeated.

Psalm 78 is a wisdom psalm that sets the stage for the teaching ministry of Y'shua. Jesus' teaching ministry was an outworking of his character and a fulfillment of this prophetic song.

Asaph wrote principally for people living in his own day, that they would learn from the experience of Israel and not repeat their errors in the days to come. But his psalm on the teaching of wisdom became as well the song of the great Teacher.

It is amazing to realize that not only the passion of the Savior was revealed in the psalms, but so was his teaching ministry. In a context of Israel's unfaithfulness (Psalm 78:9-11), the psalmist recalls God's saving acts (Psalm 78:12-16). The life and ministry of Jesus follows the same pattern.

**Manna Spurned Again**

A key point in the lengthy poem of Psalm 78 is that in spite of God's grace and constant wonders, the people still sinned and did not believe his wondrous works (Psalm 78:32). So was it also in the teaching of Jesus. Though he, the true manna of heaven, was physically present among his own people, they still sinned and did not believe.

Psalm 78 poetically recites God's deliverance of Israel from Egypt and then the perfidy of the people in the desert. The poem alternates his ongoing love (verse 38) with their continual rebellion (verse 40). Even when Yahweh had given the land to fulfill his promise (verse 55), they continued to rebel and to urge him to anger (verses 56-59).

But God remains faithful (verses 67-72). Despite the faithlessness of his people, Yahweh has still made his choice in Judah and Jerusalem, and particularly in David, his choice shepherd.

In Jesus, the good shepherd, there is one greater even than David. This we will see in the next chapter.

For now, let's assert again: Jesus is the Wise. There was never a teacher so fine as he. His teaching was rooted in the Law, was predicted in the Prophets, and is one of the songs of the book of Psalms. *Psalm 78 is a song of the Teacher* .

Now *that's* heavy!

CHAPTER
# 6

# Shepherd's Song

We have goats on our little farmlet. That's right, goats! Not smelly ones, mind you, who chew cans and jump on cars. We have beautiful French alpine dairy goats. Oh, they would chew the paper off a can and stomp on our cars if we would let them. But we don't, and our goats are beautiful. (Well, there was a time when one of our goats got into our roses, but that's another story.)

Despite the fact that I tend my goats, milk them, and groom them, I am not really a goatherd. They are my hobby, not my life. I do enjoy them. But I must admit it is a nuisance to be tied to a milk pail twice a day. My children will tell you it is more than just a nuisance to be children of a traveling speaker and be left home with dad's goats!

## Goats and Kids

On occasion, however, our goats have given us phenomenal family experiences. I'll never forget the time a few years ago when our younger son Bruce (then about five) and I were in the goat barn awaiting the birth of kids from one of our does. Bruce had asked if this time he might put the surgical glove on if the mother needed help. The glove would have gone up nearly to his shoulder! The glove wasn't needed that night.

During our long wait, Bruce asked me this question: "Daddy, do you think that when Isaac was a little boy he waited with his daddy Abraham for their goats to be born?"

That was worth a lot of milkings!

## Shepherds and Sheep

Friends of ours have sheep. I dare say they think as much of their sheep as I do of our goats. But my friends are not really shepherds any more than I am a goatherd.

It is one thing to keep an animal in a pen. It is quite another to live with and for that animal. And those are the demands placed on a genuine goatherd or shepherd.

Because of the way in which a true shepherd is so closely identified with his flock, and the flock so very dependent upon the shepherd, the writers of the Bible often speak of a king or a spiritual leader as a shepherd of his people.

We have already seen one of these lovely texts at the conclusion of Psalm 78. These words describe the transformation Yahweh did in the life of David. God took a shepherd of sheep and made him a shepherd of people:

> He chose David his servant
>> and took him from the sheep pens;
> from tending the sheep he brought him
>> to be the shepherd of his people Jacob,
>> of Israel his inheritance.
> And David shepherded them with integrity of heart;
>> with skillful hands he led them (Psalm 78: 70-72).

## False Shepherds

Writers of the Bible sometimes use the image of a false shepherd to describe evil leaders. God speaks through the prophet Zechariah in this way:

> My anger burns against the shepherds,
>> and I will punish the leaders;
> for the LORD Almighty will care
>> for his flock, the house of Judah,
>> and make them like a proud horse in battle
>>> (Zechariah 10:3).

Zechariah gives a special woe oracle to the false shepherd:

Woe to the worthless shepherd,
  who deserts the flock!
May the sword strike his arm and his right eye!
  May his arm be completely withered,
    his right eye totally blinded!
      (Zechariah 11:17).

These words of unrelieved severity show the contempt of Yahweh for a false shepherd.

## Yahweh As Shepherd

Yahweh himself is often described as the shepherd of his people, and they the flock of his pasture. The zesty praise of Psalm 100 is an example:

Know that the LORD is God.
  It is he who made us, and we are his;
  we are his people, the sheep of his pasture
    (Psalm 100:3).

Another example is the bold language of Psalm 80:1:

Hear us, O Shepherd of Israel,
  you who lead Joseph like a flock!

## The Shepherd Psalm

But whenever we think of the imagery of shepherd and sheep, we find ourselves drawn inevitably to the twenty-third psalm. That is preeminently the psalm of Yahweh as the Shepherd. Psalm 23 is also the song of the Savior who is the Good Shepherd of his sheep.

Psalm 23 is the most loved text in all of the Bible. With good reason! It is one of the loveliest of all biblical poems; the expression of faith in Yahweh it presents is a model of piety for all ages.

Fittingly, this is a psalm of David. It is not necessary to say that David wrote this poem while he was still a youthful shepherd. It may be he wrote the poem in his maturity as king of Israel. But in this poem he reflected on the experiences of his youth as well as the demands of his office. And all the while the model of Yahweh as Shepherd overwhelms him.

## Audacity of Faith

The theme of the poem is given in the first verse:

> Yahweh is my Shepherd, I do not lack
> (Psalm 23:1, personal translation; so through-
> out).

Our familiarity with these words may rob us of their audacity. It is one thing to speak of Yahweh as Rock, King, the Holy One, Creator, the Majestic. To speak of God as one's own Shepherd is exquisitely bold! The demands in this image are staggering:

- as Shepherd, the Lord must identify with his flock;
- as Shepherd, the Lord must always be near his flock;
- as Shepherd, the Lord must fight for his flock;
- as Shepherd, the Lord must be willing even to die for his flock.

*Chutzpah* is a wonderful Yiddish word that describes audacity, unmitigated gall. An old Jewish story illustrates *chutzpah*. A deranged young man kills his mother and father. When he is brought to court for his trial, he shows his chutzpah before the judge as he begs for mercy: "After all, your honor, I'm an orphan!"

It is nearly as audacious to call the eternal Yahweh "my shepherd." David does not even soften the image by using a polite plural pronoun. His boldness is heightened by the singular word "my." More expected would be the wimpy words of self-abasement that David once spoke when he was stunned by a new realization of the vastness of the universe, and his complaint that God could have no thought of him:

> What is man that you are mindful of him,
>    the son of man that you care for him?
>       (Psalm 8:4).

But in the twenty-third, David calls this same Yahweh his Shepherd! In one poem he wonders if he is just a particle on a dust cloud in a lost pocket of God's heavens. In the other poem the universe shrivels to a backdrop for the central play of all time: a shepherd walking with his sheep!

This is a psalm of confidence, a poem of absolute trust. Such a poem is remarkable when you consider the difficulty of life in ancient (and modern!) times. The psalm has the larger context of the toughness of life, but its own message is to seize on the heart of praise in the psalms: God is good! The point of this text is to emphasize the comprehensive, compassionate care Yahweh gives to his people. No more fitting image from the Semitic world was available than the shepherd and his sheep.

## Elaboration of the Theme

The thesis (verse 1) is followed by an elaboration. The question might come, just how does Yahweh meet the needs of his sheep? Verses 2-4 give some details:

> In verdant pastures he causes me to lie down,
>> by waters of quietness he gently leads me.
> He refreshes my being;
>> he leads me in ruts of righteousness,
>>> for his name's sake.
> Even if I were to walk
>> through a valley of deep darkness,
> I will not fear evil,
>> for you are with me;
> your rod and your staff,
>> they comfort me (Psalm 23:2-4).

The verbs of verses 2-4 so wonderfully express the care of God for his people. The psalmist says of God these gracious words:

- He causes me to lie down
- He leads me along carefully
- He refreshes my being
- He leads me
- He is with me
- His implements comfort me

## The Psalm in Action

A few years ago I had a wonderful experience in observing Basque shepherds caring for a huge flock of sheep. The words and images of Psalm 23 were enacted before me with stunning detail.

I was with a group of young people, mostly native American Indian believers, for an all-day excursion from our family camp near Flagstaff, Arizona. We went to a high mountain meadow situated in a caldera.

Just as we reached the rim of the high mountain and were about to descend into the depression, I shouted for the driver to stop.

Down below us it seemed the meadow was blanketed with wool. There were thousands of sheep! Apparently they had just arrived.

We got out of our buses and watched. We watched the elements of Psalm 23 enacted by modern shepherds. I would like to draw upon some of those scenes as we read the poem.

## Interlining the Poem

Let's go back over the words of verses 2-4 and interline them with comments.

### In verdant pastures he causes me to lie down.

As we watched that day in Arizona, we saw the lushness of the grass to which the shepherds brought their sheep. Round about was an arid land; there in the valley was high, green grass—a verdant meadow where these shepherds brought their sheep to feast and then to lie down to ruminate. Here was a place where the sheep could eat to their hearts' content.

### Beside waters of quietness he gently leads me.

We saw a couple of shepherds digging a trench along a fast-moving, high mountain stream. This stream was spring fed; the waters rushed along and then dropped through a fissure in the rock. When the shepherds completed the ditch, they made a connecting line from the stream. Water flowed in—and stopped. Then the sheep came to drink.

Sheep will not usually drink from fast-flowing water. They know the peril of drowning if they were to fall in and their heavy wool coats become waterlogged. They also know the danger of developing pneumonia if water gets into their lungs. Sheep have been known to die from thirst alongside abundant rushing water.

Here, these shepherds tamed the stream and gently led their sheep to the quieted waters.

### He refreshes my being.

As we watched each sheep finish drinking, one of the shepherds ran his hands quickly over the animal's body, beginning with the muzzle and working backward. It was as though the shepherd gave each sheep a quick, gentle massage.

Later, when we spoke to one of the shepherds with the aid of a Navajo interpreter, we learned these shepherds wanted to have their hands on each sheep every day. Massaging the sheep served that need for physical contact as well as providing an opportunity to check the sheep for injury, briars, or tears.

### He leads me in ruts of righteousness.

For this image, we need to leave Arizona and think of Judah. Hillsides in the Judean wilderness are scored with parallel paths moving along the contours of the hillsides. It looks like some huge hand has moved along the sides of the mountains, gouging out pathways with powerful fingers.

Once we stopped a Bedouin shepherd and spoke to him with the aid of our Arabic-speaking driver. This shepherd was on one of half a dozen paths on the hill. Behind him, walking single file, were a score of sheep.

After some polite preliminaries, we asked why it was that he was on that path and not on another.

"Because this is my path for my sheep."

"And why is this path yours?"

"Because it was my father's."

"And your father's?"

"It was his father's path before him. This has always been our family's path."

"And that path over there?"

"That's the path of Abu-issa."

"And the path down there?"

"That's the path of Ibrahim."

Each path was the path of a particular shepherd. As he would walk his path, his sheep would follow along behind in single file, keeping to the right rut.

With no shepherd the sheep would scatter all over the hillside. They would not be in the right rut at all and would soon become prey for all manner of harmful, hungry creatures.

### For his name's sake.

The psalm begins arrestingly with the bold statement that Yahweh is my shepherd. After David has recorded some of Yahweh's acts of care that mark him as the Good Shepherd, he points to the outworking of God's name.

That is, all of God's gracious acts fit his character. His name is a name of relationship. His name is a mark of constancy. His name reveals his relatedness to his people.

It is because of who he is, as revealed in his name Yahweh, that the Lord takes such care of his flock.

### Even though I may walk in a valley of deep darkness.

The traditional reading of this line, of course, is "the valley of the shadow of death." On occasion there will be tour guides in Israel who will point out a narrow ravine that may be seen in the distance as one travels the road from Jericho to Jerusalem. Some guides call this "the valley of the shadow of death." They indicate that it was this very spot that David had in mind. They then go on to tell of brigands who stalk that pathway even today.

Tourists whip out their new Nikons and try to focus on

that distant ravine, thinking, "Wait till I show the folks back home!"

Trying to take a photo of "the" valley of the shadow of death is akin to taking a picture of the spot where crumbs might have fallen when the Lord divided the loaves and the fishes.

The Hebrew word translated "shadow of death" is problematic. Recent studies in Ugaritic, a language of the Canaanite peoples from the early biblical period, suggest that this Hebrew word is to be pronounced *ṣalmûṯ* rather than *ṣalmāweṯ*, and is to be translated "deep darkness" rather than "shadow of death."

This text does not limit the care of the shepherd for his sheep only to the passage marred by death. Any valley of deep darkness is an opportunity for the special care of the shepherd. Psalm 23 is too often relegated to the funeral service; it is a psalm of life!

### I fear no evil; you are with me.

The psalmist does not deny the reality of evil. Rather, he affirms that in the presence of evil there is nothing to be feared . . . if one is also in the presence of God.

There is no word so comforting in the Bible than the word of divine presence to aid and help in time of need.

Remember the story of Joseph being cast into a prison in Egypt? There he was in a dungeon in Egypt only because he had been faithful to his master, his God, and himself.

There he was in a hole. But the narrator then says, "But Yahweh was with him" (Genesis 39:21). There, in the cell, even there he was not alone. Even there he knew the presence of God.

When a person really knows the presence of God in his life, then it is possible to say with David—and with believers from Joseph through Peter, from biblical times to our own day—"I fear no evil at all; Yahweh is with me!"

### Your rod and staff, they comfort me.

That day we watched the shepherds in Arizona, a shepherd on the opposite bank rushed to his jeep at one point to grab his rifle. He pointed to the opposite bank from which we were watching and shot. Likely he had seen some animal lurking in the distance, waiting a chance to get near a stray sheep or a weak lamb.

The shepherd had seen the enemy. But the sheep went on about their business, quite unconcerned about the whole affair. After all, when the shepherd is on duty, the sheep are safe.

Ancient shepherds didn't have rifles. They had two implements, one for defense and one for care. The rod was a club which the shepherd might use to drive off a wolf or a lioness. The staff is the traditional shepherd's cane with the hook on one end. Should a lamb fall off into a crevasse, the shepherd might be able to reach down with his crook and hook it around the legs and chest and pull it to safety.

The theme of the psalm is confirmed by these several mercies of the Shepherd to his sheep. The poem describes the theme. When Yahweh is Shepherd, one does not want. With Yahweh as Shepherd, the implements at his hand are limitless and his care is boundless.

## Sheep and Banquet

This may surprise you, but some readers of Psalm 23 think the last section (verses 5-6) does not fit well with the rest of the poem. It seems, they say, that the image of the shepherd and sheep radically changes to a new image of host and guest. They speak of the poem's discontinuity rather than its unity.

On my own part, I think the poem shows marvelous unity. The problem is with too literal an interpretation of figurative language. Verse 5 appears to be an example of hyperbole, of deliberate exaggeration for rhetorical effect. The poet continues to think of shepherd and sheep, but now his imagination is boundless as he describes the supreme care he receives as the sheep of such a caring shepherd.

He begins in verse 5 to picture the sheep as a guest at a banquet and the shepherd as host. It is the same imagery, but now enhanced and extended to show in the most forceful way how wonderful the care of the shepherd really is:

You arrange before me a table,
    in the presence of my enemies;
You anoint with oil my head,
    my cup is overflowing!
        (Psalm 23:5)

## Let the Beasts Look On

The pasture has been glorified to a table, exquisitely spread with the finest utensils. Ancient equivalents of linen, china, silver, and crystal are intended. Grass becomes a banquet feast, water an expensive wine, olive oil meant for the sheep's wounds is transformed into gracious refreshment for a weary and dusty traveler come to a sumptuous dinner.

And all the while, on the rim of the meadow, hungry and salivating carnivores look on from a distance. Let them look! They shan't get anything more than a sniff! Let them look. Let them wish they were sheep of the shepherd rather than dogs of the desert! Let them look, and let them weep. Let tears join saliva. Let them look!

It is still sheep and shepherd.
    But the care is exquisite.
        Such a Shepherd!

## Tomorrow and Forever

And the future? Secure as the present! The last line culminates the poem: Yahweh's care for his sheep extends through this life to the life to come:

Surely goodness and loyal love will pursue me
    all the days of my life,
and I will dwell in the house of Yahweh
    forever (Psalm 23:6).

The life of a sheep with a careless shepherd is fragile indeed. But the life of a sheep with the Good Shepherd is marked so fully by his attending grace that these sheep are no longer even chased by wolves and dogs. They are *pursued* (the literal meaning of the verb usually translated "will follow me") by the goodness and loving loyalty of their Shepherd. He, the Shepherd, now hunts me with his goodness! He, the Shepherd, now chases after me with his loyal love!

Such is the dramatic beauty of this imagery.

And it is both for today *and* for the life to come. All the days of my life I am in the care of this shepherd. And in the days that will come, I will be in his house forever. The sheep-fold becomes a picture of the heavenly home for the child of God. Even critical scholars are coming to realize that the last line of this poem speaks of eternal life.

## The Psalm As a Prayer

As we think over this poem we may observe two great things about it. It is a prayer; it is also a model.

When we approach the psalm as a prayer, we know that in the first place it was the personal prayer of David to Yahweh. David knew shepherding from the back side of the sheep. But now he pictured himself as a sheep and Yahweh as his shepherd. In this psalm he expressed his trust in the Good Shepherd and his prayer that the Shepherd ever remain true.

Psalm 23 is similarly the confession of trust and the prayer for continuity of care that may be expressed by any believer in the Lord. This is why the poem was made a part of the hymnal of Israel. It is not just David who prayed and trusted in this way. All genuine believers may express the same strong beauty of praise to God.

## The Prayer of Y'shua the Lamb

Yet in the final sense, Psalm 23 is the prayer of Jesus to Yahweh. It is his prayer of confidence in the time of his humanity. *For he was the lamb!* When John the Baptist saw Y'shua coming to him he said, "Look, the Lamb of God, who takes away the sin of the world!" (John 1:29, see also verse 36).

Psalm 23 is thus the perfect prayer for Y'shua during his humanity. He had come as the Lamb of God, the Lamb of Passover (1 Corinthians 5:7). During his life as Lamb, he must have addressed his Father regularly in the imagery of shepherd. In fact, as we shall see in our study of Psalm 22, the Shepherd imagery came to a head in the suffering of the Lamb on the cross.

John's visions of the worship of Y'shua in heaven present him as Lamb, the Lamb who is altogether worthy. All of heaven burst into glorious song, the song of the Lamb:

> Worthy is the Lamb, who was slain,
> to receive power and wealth and
>    wisdom and strength
> and honor and glory and praise!
>
> To him who sits on the throne and to the Lamb
>    be praise and honor and glory and power,
>       for ever and ever!
>          (Revelation 5:12-13).

## The Psalm As Model

The twenty-third is not only a psalm of confident prayer. It is also a model of what the true shepherd really is. The true shepherd (and the true goatherd) does a great deal more than just keep sheep and goats. He lives for the sheep. He tends the sheep fully. He meets their needs in ways fully suited to them.

When David became king of Israel, it was on the model of shepherding, as Psalm 78:70-72 declares. All that David said of the Lord as his Shepherd was a model for him in caring for the people of his pasture.

Moreover, as we have already seen in texts relating to false shepherds, the model of the good shepherd extends to all human rulers, and particularly to those who would tend the flock of God. In the New Testament, one word used for spiritual leaders is *pastor*. The pastor is shepherd; the model is Yahweh.

## The Model of Y'shua the Shepherd

Psalm 23 is particularly the model for Y'shua as the Shepherd of his people. This is why the New Testament can use the wonderful interplay of images. Jesus is the Lamb of God; he is also the Good Shepherd.

Psalm 23 becomes the song of the Savior which he sings best in John 10. Jesus' words, "I am the good shepherd" (John 10:11, 14), are a bold and full application to himself of Psalm 23. A reflective reader would have been stunned at the words of Y'shua here. This is as bold as his assertion to be the divine "I AM" in John 8:58. When Jesus calls himself the good shepherd, he is identifying himself with Yahweh in the Shepherd Psalm.

But in the audacity there is also a mark of his humiliation. When he calls himself shepherd, it is in the context of being willing to die for his sheep. Observe again these words:

- "I am the good shepherd. The good shepherd lays down his life for the sheep" (John 10:11).
- "I am the good shepherd; I know my sheep and my sheep know me—just as the Father knows me and I know the Father—and I lay down my life for the sheep" (John 10:14-15).
- "The reason my Father loves me is that I lay down my life—only to take it up again. No one takes it from me, but I lay it down of my own accord. . . . This command I received from my father" (John 10:17-18).

These words are marvelous. Jesus declares that he is the good shepherd, but that in his case it is a mark of death. For this is a shepherd who will have to die for his sheep. But he dies of his own accord, and he promises to live again.

Here are the elements of the gospel: Y'shua dies for his own, and then he rises in newness of life. And Jesus built this statement of the gospel from the song of the shepherd, his song—Psalm 23.

**Responses to Y'shua**

The responses of the people in that day (see John 10:19-21) are not dissimilar to our own. There are three options: (1) He is demon-possessed, and is therefore dangerous; (2 he is stark-raving mad and is therefore pitiable; or (3) he speaks truth which is life itself.

Which conclusion have you made concerning Y'shua who calls himself the Good Shepherd?

## The Shepherd of the Kingdom

The song of the Shepherd points to the future for the believer who commits his or her life to the mercy of that shepherd. The image of Y'shua as the good shepherd points to the future as well.

The goal of the prophetic word is that the Lord Jesus Christ be revealed as the great Shepherd of his people. Remember the words of the prophet Micah? These were given in the same passage as the famed birth-in-Bethlehem prophecy:

> He will stand and shepherd his flock
>     in the strength of the LORD,
>     in the majesty of the name of the LORD his
> God.
> And they will live securely, for then his greatness
>     will reach to the ends of the earth.
>     And he will be their peace (Micah 5:4-5).

There is no more lovely picture than this! Y'shua is the Good Shepherd. *He is the singer of the Shepherd's Song.*

When we turn to Psalm 23 for our own pleasure and comfort, we are turning to a song we share with Y'shua.

That beats keeping goats in the backyard. Anytime!

# 7

---

# Passover
# Song

**I**t was one of these evenings that change one's life. As seems so often the case, we had no idea how important the night would be at the time.

Ralph and Myrna Alexander had invited Beverly and me to their home for a special dinner. The dinner was the celebration of the Jewish Passover *Seder*. That night opened up a new world for us, a world we are still exploring and learning to enjoy more fully.

Since that time, the Alexanders and the Allens, along with a number of others, have continued to celebrate Passover each year during the Christian Holy Week. We do this both at home and with many groups of Christian people.

Questions come, of course. The words "Jewish Passover during Christian Holy Week" seem like a strange mishmash. To rephrase an old Jewish joke, some wonder what a nice Christian boy is doing with that funny little hat on his head.

**Christian Values in a Jewish Feast**

We have found several values in our participation in this Jewish feast:

- First, the value that the Passover ceremony has for the family to learn together.
- Second, the splendid opportunity the festival gives for Christian families to learn to appreciate the positive values of Jewish tradition.

- Third, without question the most significant aspect of the Passover *Seder* (ceremony) is its associations in the life of the Savior Y'shua.

## A Family Affair

Passover is essentially a family affair. Among other things, this is a special time for the family to put into practice the familial aspects of the Law of Moses. What a special time for parents to teach diligently the great works of Yahweh in the history of Israel! The Passover festival is the annual recitation of the events of God's great deliverance of Israel from Egypt.

This is the central story of the Hebrew Bible. It is a story Christian families need to learn just as surely as Jewish families.

## Down with the Walls

The wall of separation between Christians and Jews has been in place too long. Let's do away with the wall! Let's realize how important Jewish contributions are to our faith.

We dare not deny genuine differences, of course! We do not wish to dull the edge of the gospel or to downplay the centrality of our faith in Y'shua the Messiah. We will not ignore reality "just to be nice." It's really *not* nice!

There are some Christian groups which, in striving to build relationships with Jewish people (a commendable act), refuse to mention the name of Jesus (or Y'shua!) to Jews unless they are specifically asked. They feel this is a means to remove the offense of the gospel of Jesus.

But not to speak of Jesus to Jews is the unkindest act of all. We may call it a form of anti-Semitism—perhaps the worst! For if all Christians stopped witnessing of their faith in Jesus to Jews, we would effectively remove God's ancient people from the hearing of God's good news.

At the same time, in those areas where our own faith and understanding may be enriched by contacts with Jewish traditions, let's move on and "get with the program!" Dr. Joe Aldrich has urged Christians to learn how to draw lines of grace when it comes to Christian interaction with

Jewish people. "If lines must be drawn," he says, "let them be drawn *around* us rather than between us."

## Y'shua and Passover

The Gospels mark out several times in the life of Y'shua when he came to Jerusalem to celebrate the Passover. Two times interest us the most. The first is the celebration of the Passover with his family when he was twelve years old (Luke 2:42).

This was not unusual for the family of Jesus. The text states explicitly that the family went to Jerusalem for the Feast of the Passover every year (Luke 2:41). This was a particularly important occasion for the Lord Y'shua. It was also a very difficult time for his mother and a time of astonishment for the masters of Torah in the temple. We must not forget that the family of Jesus regularly participated in the Passover, and that this story comes in that context. It was a godly family into which Y'shua had been born. The celebration of the Passover was a mark of their piety.

## His Last Passover

Most significant, of course, is the *last* time our Savior celebrated the Passover. This was on the night of his betrayal. It was on the eve of his crucifixion. This was the last night of his life.

Think of it! Had you been in the sandals of the Lord, what would you have done on the last night of your life? This is what he did: Y'shua began that night with his disciples clustered around the Passover table.

It was on that night that Y'shua took the second sheet of *matsa*, broke it, and told his disciples that this bread of mystery was the potent symbol of his own body. Just as he broke the bread, so his own body was about to be broken.

## The Bread

The commandment to eat *matsa*, unleavened bread, came from Moses to the people of Israel as a part of their instructions for the first Passover (Exodus 12:1-28). The bread was to be made without yeast, to emphasize the haste of the departure of the people from Egypt

(Deuteronomy 16:3, "because you left Egypt in haste").

The Old Testament made several strict demands respecting the celebration of the Passover. These concerned the eating of the lamb, the bitter herbs, and the unleavened bread. It was later tradition that prescribed that there be three sheets of *matsa* bread on ceremonial display and that the second of the three sheets was to be broken into two pieces. We do not really know how soon these traditions developed.

What we do know is that all their lives the disciples had taken the second of the three sheets of *matsa* and had then broken this sheet into two pieces. The one half would be hidden away. Then it would be found after the meal and be brought back so that the two pieces might be held together. All would see how the two irregular halves would fit together magnificently. Then this bread would be eaten as the *Afikomen*, the dessert.

Then on this night, their master did something quite unexpected. He explained the real meaning of the breaking of the bread! The breaking of the unleavened bread is a symbol of the death he was to suffer. The fitting together of the pieces is a symbol of the life he would live again.

How very lovely this is! One of the most important elements of the Old Testament faith becomes one of the most important elements of the New Testament faith. By this master stroke, Y'shua tied together the saving acts of Yahweh from both testaments. He who provided bread in the period of the Hebrew wanderings has become the bread of life in the New Testament period. The "bread of [their] affliction"—the Old Testament description (Deuteronomy 16:3)—was now the symbol of his affliction.

**The Cup**

Then he took the cup. How many times have we participated in the Lord's table and have heard the words concerning the cup, but have never thought of the importance of the definite article, "*the* cup"?

During the Passover meal there are four cups of wine, two before the meal and two after. The third cup is "the cup of salvation"—how appropriate a name for the cup our Savior raised!

But there may be something more. Perhaps the definite article points not just to the third cup, but to another cup altogether.

It was the cup of Elijah, the special cup filled with wine at the beginning of the feast in anticipation that perhaps this might be the night that Elijah, the prophet of blessed memory, might join the family in their sacred feast.

This would fulfill the words of the prophet Malachi, the last promise of the Hebrew Bible:

> See, I will send you the prophet Elijah before that great and dreadful day of the LORD comes. He will turn the hearts of the fathers to their children, and the hearts of the children to their fathers; or else I will come and strike the land with a curse (Malachi 4:5-6).

It would anticipate the coming of the Promised One, concerning whom all the Hebrew Bible speaks with growing delight, that the cup of Elijah would be filled. The cup of Elijah was a potent Messianic symbol.

Normally, however, at the end of the meal, the cup would be emptied. No one would drink from it. Elijah had not come. Messiah was not here. The cup would be cleansed in hope of another year.

"Next year. Next year!"

**This Year**

*This* was the year!

Messiah has come!

The cup is ours to drink from!

He has told us, "Each of you drink from it."

It is difficult for us who are so far removed from that day fully to realize the unexpectedness of this moment. The celebration of the Lord's Table in the context of the Passover *Seder* gives us the best opportunity to imagine their horror the next day when the impact of his death came crashing home.

It was only on Sunday that they bathed in delicious joy as he stood before them again and explained all over all the things that the Scriptures had said to prepare them for such a moment.

**Their Songs**

When our Lord and his disciples reclined that night at the low table, certain things were expected. The Passover was done "in order"—the meaning of the Hebrew word *seder*.

We know that a number of psalms were sung at the Passover feast. Psalms 113-114 were sung before the festive meal; Psalms 115-118 afterward, with the Great Hallel, Psalm 136, at the climax.

The New Testament even tells us of their singing that night: "When they had sung a hymn, they went out to the Mount of Olives" (Matthew 26:30). Sometimes in our churches we read this verse and then sing, "Blest Be the Tie That Binds." This is a fine hymn, but was not the song that Jesus sang with his disciples that night. Actually, we know what the music was: They sang the psalms of Passover.

**Songs for Jesus to Sing**

Think of how some words of these ancient hymns must have leaped from the pages of their memory as they sang them that night. Think of these songs especially as *Songs for Jesus to Sing*. We may gain some understanding of these hymns if we *think Jesus* as we read the words.

**Struggle with Death**

Psalm 116 describes the psalmist's struggle with the thought of death. These are his words:

> The cords of death entangled me,
>> the anguish of the grave came upon me;
>> I was overcome by trouble and sorrow.
> Then I called on the name of the LORD;
>> "O LORD, save me!" (Psalm 116:3-4).

Then the psalmist proclaims his utter confidence in Yahweh (verses 5-7) and his faith in God's deliverance:

For you, O LORD, have delivered my
    soul from death,
      my eyes from tears,
that I may walk before the LORD
    in the land of the living (Psalm 116:8-9).

What must have been going through the mind of our Lord as he said these words that night!

- He knew he was facing death.
- He knew he would live again.

The words of this psalm emboldened him for the raw reality of death ahead and encouraged him with the sweet wonder of victory over the enemy of us all. Was it not in part because of the teaching of this psalm in his life that he, "for the joy set before him endured the cross, scorning its shame"? (Hebrews 12:2).

The apostle Paul understood that Psalm 116 prophesied the hope of Messiah in his own resurrection. Paul quotes Psalm 116:10 in 2 Corinthians 4:13-15:

It is written: "I believed; therefore I have spoken."
With that same spirit of faith we also believe and
therefore speak, because we know that the one
who raised the Lord Jesus from the dead will
also raise us with Jesus and present us with you
in his presence.

The words of this psalm, therefore, give not only the hope of Jesus for his life beyond death; this psalm is designed to give us confidence for life beyond the grave as well.

## The Cup of Salvation

Again we wonder: What would it have been like to have been present that night and to have heard Y'shua sing his psalms? Y'shua is Lord of song. The psalms belong to him. They are the libretto of his passion, the songs of his life.

Psalm 116:12-14 presents the strong image of raising the cup of salvation:

> How can I repay the LORD
>   for all his goodness to me?
> I will lift up the cup of salvation
>   and call on the name of the LORD.
> I will fulfill my vows to the LORD
>   in the presence of all his people.

Can you see it? Jesus reaches out his own hand as he sings these words. He grasps the cup of Elijah, holds it high, raising the cup in blessing to God. All the while he knew *within* that this cup was a symbol of his blood. All the while he knew that this cup would only become the cup of salvation if he were to be faithful to the Father and proceed to the cross.

There he holds the cup. Angels of heaven shrink back. There he holds the cup. His father in heaven is grieved at the thought. There he holds the cup. And because he holds it high, we may live forever!

## Precious Death

With cup held high, the thought of death paramount on his mind, the Savior's thoughts must have gone to the next words of this intensely messianic psalm:

> Precious in the sight of the LORD
>   is the death of his saints.
> O LORD, truly I am your servant;
>   I am your servant, the son of your maid-
>   servant;
>   you have freed me from my chains (Psalm
> 116:15-16).

We have no idea who wrote Psalm 116; the poem is anonymous. Whoever it was, the poet had great insight into the heart of God. When one of God's saints (the Hebrew word has the connotation of devout faithfulness) dies, there is grief on the part of the Father above. When the one who dies is an especially trusted servant, the grief of the Father is compounded. But when the one who died was the altogether wonderful one, the Lord Y'shua, then we may truly say that there was grieving in all of heaven. This psalm gives the words for the Savior to sing as he acknowledged his understanding of his Father's grief at the suffering that lay before him.

Isn't it touching to read in this psalm the reference to blessed Mary as well? "I [Y'shua] am your servant, the son of your maidservant [Mary]."

All of this points to the cross. It points to the Savior hanging there. It points to his Father grieving there. It points to his mother in grief there as well. What a scene this is! The most amazing thing is that the words describing this scene were written as a hymn for Israel to sing, hundreds of years before the Savior would sing them with his disciples for their fullest meaning.

**The Savior's Praise**

The last words of verse 16 point to deliverance. We do not know what that deliverance was for the psalmist. We *do* know what it was for the Savior. It was life! It was resurrection! It was deliverance from death, victory over the grave, defeat of the evil one, salvation for his people.

And when it was all done, then the Savior, as the psalmist, turns to the father with praise:

> I will sacrifice a thank offering to you
>    and call on the name of the LORD.
> I will fulfill my vows to the LORD
>    in the presence of all his people,
> in the courts of the house of the LORD—
>    in your midst, O Jerusalem.
> *Praise the* LORD (Psalm 116:17-19)

Here are the words of the Savior in his vow to praise God when the salvation work of the cross was over and when God would have made him the victor. We will see this theme again in other of the psalms of the Passion. Every time we see it, however, it is remarkable. Jesus' faith in his Father was profound; the words he used to state that faith were found in the psalms of Passover he sang with his disciples that night as they celebrated the feast together.

**Passover Song**

Perhaps the most remarkable song of all that night was the singing of Psalm 118. This is the quintessential

Passover song. Psalm 118, like Psalm 116, is an anonymous poem. Whoever wrote it must have been profoundly moved by the Spirit of God. The words the poet used to describe his own distress became the special words of the Savior. If ever there were a mark of the inspiration of the Bible, it is in prophetic psalms such as Psalm 118.

Psalm 118 was given over to the congregation of Israel to sing in worship in the holy temple. The psalm begins and concludes with the central thesis of the book of Psalms:

> Give thanks to the LORD, for he is good;
>     his love endures forever (Psalm 118:1, 29).

These words express a deep heart of praise to Yahweh, God of Israel. Unlike the supposed deities of their neighbors—deities who were evil, capricious, malevolent, petty, and vindictive—Yahweh is *good*! When Israel thought rightly about God, she praised him that he is good and that his loyal love (Hebrew, *ḥesed*) endures forever.

There is more to it than just the words, however. The first four verses of the psalm call for all members of the worshiping community to join in praise to Yahweh, whose *ḥesed*, loyal love, endures forever.

Between the Invocation (Psalm 118:1-4) and the Doxology (verses 28-29), there are six distinct sections to this psalm:

- A Report of Deliverance (verses 5-9)
- The Drama of Deliverance (verses 10-14)
- The Purpose of Deliverance (verses 15-18)
- The Praise of the Delivered One (verses 19-21)
- The Surprise of Deliverance (verses 22-24)
- The Continuity of Deliverance (verses 25-27)

**Yahweh Is for Me**

I suspect one of the most important things one can know in a time of great trouble is that the Lord is with him. When Joseph was in prison, Yahweh was with him. When Daniel was in the lion's den, Yahweh was with him. When the psalmist was in terrible trouble that brought deep anguish to him, he could say that the Lord was with him.

In fact, the Hebrew wording of verse 6 is even stronger than saying "the Lord is with me." The Hebrew says "Yahweh is *for* me!" The care of God is pointed my way, says the psalmist. He exists for my good. This is not an egocentric statement; it is the proper stance of faith. *This is the meaning of his name.* The eternal Yahweh has declared that he is *for his people* (Exodus 3:12-15; 6:2-9).

While the active presence of Yahweh is a genuine reality in the life of all of his people, it would be particularly true in the life—and death—of the Savior Y'shua. There is nothing better in all of life than to take one's refuge in Yahweh. With the Lord *for* me, of whom shall I be afraid?

> Yahweh is for me, my glorious helper.
> I will look in triumphal disdain on my enemies!
> (Psalm 118:7, personal translation).

**The Surprise of God**

Psalm 118:10-14 describes the drama of deliverance in the life of the psalmist. He speaks in exaggerated language of the overwhelming attack upon him by his enemies.

In three verses he describes their assault upon him:

- All nations surround me.
- They surround me completely.
- They surround me like bees, as burning thorns (Psalm 118:10-12, personal translation).

But in each of these verses, he expresses his resolute triumph, based on the active presence of Yahweh:

- but in the name Yahweh I cut them off!

The words of surprise come in verses 13-14. The assault of his enemies was so terrible there was danger that the psalmist might have been defeated after all. He was pushed back; it seemed he was about to fall. But then Yahweh helped him. And when he was helped by God, he was like the people of Israel when the armies of Pharaoh pursued them right up to the banks of the Red Sea. With the sea before them and the armies of Egypt behind them, there seemed to be no deliverance at all.

*Then God stooped down!*

Then Yahweh burst in.

The Lord destroyed the power of the sea before them; the Lord defeated the power of the army behind them.

- The sea he drove back by the blast of his nostrils.
- The army he drowned by the waters he unleashed.

## Miriam's Song

The central words of the great hymn of Miriam and Moses (Exodus 15),commemorating the central saving event of the Hebrew Bible, are these:

> The LORD is my strength and my song;
> he has become my salvation.
> He is my God, and I will praise him,
> my father's God, and I will exalt him.
> The LORD is a warrior;
> the LORD is his name (Exodus 15:2-3).

A more literal rendering of the first two lines:

> My strong song is Yah;
> and *he* has become my salvation!

These are the very words of our writer in Psalm 118:14. They are the central motif of the song of salvation. These words are the basic declaration of the delivered.

## At the Table of Y'shua

Now again, *think* Y'shua! Remember him as the singer of these words, as he and his disciples reclined at the feast-laden table. He had held out the bread and had broken it. He had grasped the cup and had passed it over to his friends. Though they still had not caught on fully, *he knew*.

- He knew what the night would bring.
- He knew what the day would bring.

But he also knew what God would bring. He knew that out of his dying would come an opportunity for great praise to God. For he knew he would not be left to linger in death.

God, who had extended his right hand to save Israel from Egypt, would surely extend his right hand to save his son from death.

Hence, the triplet of confidence:

The right hand of Yahweh does mighty things!
The right hand of Yahweh is exalted;
The right hand of Yahweh does mighty things!
(Psalm 118:15c-16, personal translation)

Then Y'shua the singer, using the libretto prepared for him hundreds of years earlier in this psalm, was able to say:

I will not die but live,
and I will proclaim the works of Yah!
Though Yah will have chastened me severely,
he will not have given me over utterly to death
(Psalm 118:17-18, personal translation).

Did these words mean that he would not die? Certainly not. He knew he would die. These words meant he would *live* even though he were to die.

Since he knew he would live, Y'shua knew also that he would praise God among his friends again. We will see more of these themes when we move to the psalms of victory.

**The Cornerstone**

Among the most cherished words of the psalms in apostolic preaching are the words describing the surprising action of God in taking a rejected stone and using it for the cornerstone.

Think of a stonemason at work. He picks up a stone, hacks off an unseemly lump, then fits the stone into the building. At one point he tosses aside a stone he deems unfit for use.

- Then the hand of God swoops down.
- Then the surprise of Yahweh bursts in.

The hand of God takes the rejected stone and makes it the stone of the cap position:

> The stone the builders rejected
> has become the capstone (Psalm 118:22).

This verse is cited repeatedly in the New Testament of the surprise of our Savior (Matthew 21:42; Mark 12:10-11; Luke 20:17; Acts 4:11; Ephesians 2:20; 1 Peter 2:7).

The delight of the Father is to surprise his people by glorifying his Son. The work was his alone; we share in his delight:

> From Yahweh this is done;
> it is wonderful in our eyes! (Psalm 118:23,
> personal translation).

When we think rightly about it, we recognize that the resurrection day of the Savior is the central day in all of history. For it is *this* day in which we find the most compelling call to joy:

> This is the day Yahweh has made,
> Let us be exceedingly happy in it (Psalm
> 118:24, personal translation).

We have sung the words of this verse many times. Perhaps we have not seen the setting of the words before in the context of this psalm. "This is the day that the Lord has made/we will rejoice and be glad in it," is an appropriate sentiment for any day of our life in faith. But it is especially in the context of the Savior's song of hope in Yahweh on the eve of his death that these words have their ultimate meaning.

The Hebrew for "we will rejoice" is the word *nagîlâ*. Here is where Jewish people have learned to sing *Hava Nagila*, "Come, Let Us Rejoice!" Our rejoicing is in Y'shua! Many sing of being happy who have yet to know the joy of God in the deliverance of Y'shua from death—and because of his deliverance, the good news of *our* deliverance from the power of death as well.

## Hosanna

One thing remains in this psalm—and it is the most haunting of all. We are familiar with the procession of our Lord into the holy city of Jerusalem on Palm Sunday. We know the crowd shouted "Hosanna!" and "Blessed is he who comes in the name of the Lord!" (Matthew 21:9). What we may not know is that these words of the crowd that day came from our psalm:

> O LORD, save us;
>> O LORD, grant us success.
> Blessed is he who comes in the name of the LORD.
>> From the house of the LORD we bless you
>> (Psalm 118:25-26).

The words "O LORD, save us" read this way in Hebrew: *ānnā' 'adōnay, hôshî 'â nā'*. When the crowd sang these words, they were singing the song of Psalm 118. Some tried to stop them from their song. Y'shua said that if the people stopped their praise, the very rocks would have to shout them (Luke 19:40). That is how significant these words were to our Lord!

He had entered the city to save his people. As he entered, the populace shouted the words of this psalm. Now, on the eve of his salvation work, he sang these words with his disciples.

Then they went out to the Mount of Olives.

Next time you are at a communion service, think a bit about these things. Think about the songs our Savior sang when he broke the bread and when he held out the cup.

Y'shua *is* the singer of the psalms. And his psalms of Passover are among the most impressive.

# 8

# Passion Song

**I**t was the next day. The long night was finally over; but it was no mercy. The light of day had brought the worst pain of all.

There he hangs!

Suspended.

Alone.

There are others there; but he is alone in a way he has never known.

This time, God is gone.

And there he hangs.

## In the Garden

The night had been interminable. One pain after another. He had gone to the garden in Gat Shemen, the oil press in the olive grove on the hill east of the city. His inner pain had been such that he confided to Peter, James, and John that he was overwhelmed with a depression that had him on the point of death.

He prayed that night. He fell to the ground and prayed as even he had never prayed before. He prayed the Father might remove the cup from him. Though he had held the cup of salvation high and had sung about it earlier, now it seemed too much. Yet his prayer was ever to do the will of his Father.

During those intense moments of praying, his disciples had fallen asleep. None had even stayed awake to pray for him in his utter distress.

Again he went off to pray. Again he beseeched the Father to remove the cup of suffering from him. Again he committed himself to the Father's will. Again he returned to sleeping disciples.

Things were done by threes that night. The third time he went off to pray, he did not even try to arouse his friends. He went to pray alone. His distress was such that he spoke to God in Aramaic, the language of his home, the language of his mother. "Abba!" he screamed, using the Aramaic term for father. And as he prayed more earnestly it seemed as though his perspiration became great drops of blood falling to the ground.

He went back to his friends, roused them, and warned them of the trouble to come.

**His Trial**

He was betrayed. It was a friend, done by a kiss.

He was denied. It was a friend, done with an oath. Three times.

He was beaten. They mocked him. They beat him again. They gave him a crown, but it was made of sharp thorns. They gave him a scepter, but it was a stick. They robed him in purple and gave him homage, but it was the cruel joke of bored soldiers.

He went through mock trials, all illegal, yet deadly serious. There were three settings, back and forth: the Sanhedrin, Pilate, Herod, then Pilate again.

He was never proven guilty of anything. He was just sentenced to death.

**His Dying**

They made him carry the cross-bar. He was so weakened by the terrors of the night that he stumbled and fell. Another was conscripted to carry it for him.

Then they nailed him to the cross. Large, rough spikes pierced his wrists and his ankles. They lifted him up and dropped the cross home. With a thunk that tore at his wounds, he was thrust forward into the cruel punishment that was not unusual in that day for a terrible criminal or an insidious rebel. Things were still done in threes: Two thieves died beside him.

Rarely would a good man die so terribly.
  Never one so good as he.
There he hangs.
  Suspended.
    Alone.
      Even God is gone.
The hours pass. But they pass more slowly than time has ever moved. Pain pervades his body so fully, language is mute.

An unnatural darkness covers the place in the middle of the day. Heaven blushes to see such a sight.

At one point, he screams out words in Aramaic. The words were strong and clear to him; but down below, so far away, the words were misunderstood. They thought he was calling " *Eliyahu*," (Elijah). They took this as a new occasion to mock him. "Look at that! He's near death, but he still hasn't given up on his crazy dreams. He's screaming for Elijah to come to deliver him! What a pity."

He hadn't called for Elijah. It is just that so far below, his word sounded like that. He was calling for one far more important than the prophet of blessed memory. He was calling out for his God.

It was not *Eliyahu* that he had said, but E*loi*. Twice he said "Eloi." This is the Aramaic word, "My God!" Twice he said, "My God." Then he added the words, "*Lama sabachthani?*" (Matthew 27:46; Mark 15:34). What he had screamed was, "My God! Why have you forsaken me?"

**His Scream of Pain**

It seems uncanny. In a way it is difficult to believe. The psalms were not only the libretto for the Savior on the last night of his life as he sang with his disciples at Passover feast. The psalms were also the libretto for his dying. These words of pain were from the psalms.

When the Savior Y'shua was suspended there on the cross, bearing the pain of physical suffering of a terrible death, he turned once more to the psalms. Again he reached out to prophetic song to express the depths of his soul. Even on the cross, it was music!

But why *that* music? Why that song? Why the scream of desertion? Why the call of terror?

It was more than the physical pain. It was more than the agony of his body. It was because of what he had become. It was because of the distancing of God from his hurt.

So he screamed, "Eloi! Eloi!" But he heard no voice, he sensed no answer.

There he hangs.

Suspended.

Alone.

Even God is gone.

## What He Had Become

He had *become* sin, you know. This was not just a good man who died unjustly. That is always sad, but it has happened before, and likely will happen again. Nor was he a man who suffered the most terrible form of physical pain that ever a man has borne. I suspect that as unbearable as the death of Y'shua was, there have been those who have died even more painful deaths.

The most awful thing about his death was that he became *sin*. He, who had never committed a breach of Torah, who had kept faithfully the inner essence of the law to God's perfect satisfaction—he was made to be sin itself as he died that day on the cross.

Years after the death of Y'shua, the apostle Paul explained his death in this way: "God made him [Y'shua] who had no sin to be sin for us, so that in him we might become the righteousness of God" (2 Corinthians 5:21). It was what he had *become* that was so very terrible.

## Isaiah's Song

This was all a part of the plan of God from the beginning. Hundreds of years before Y'shua died, God revealed his plan through the great prophet Isaiah. These are his words. They are among the most wonderful in all of the prophets. They present the meaning of the death Y'shua, God's Servant, would die, seven hundred years before he hung there suspended that day.

106

Surely he took up our infirmities
  and carried our sorrows,
yet we considered him stricken by God,
  smitten by him, and afflicted
But he was pierced for our transgressions,
  he was crushed for our iniquities;
the punishment that brought us peace was upon
him,
  and by his wounds we are healed.
We all, like sheep, have gone astray,
  each of us has turned to his own way;
and the LORD has laid on him
  the iniquity of us all (Isaiah 53:4-6).

## Where Jesus Walked

I walked today where Jesus walked. At least I was in the near vicinity of where he walked. At times I was on a level of the city high above the plane of the city of Jesus' day. At times I was meters one way or another from the path he walked. But I was near. I was very near.

I stood again on the *lithostratos*, the stone pavement where Jesus stood before Pilate, where he was cruelly mocked and finally condemned to die.

I walked all through the Church of the Holy Sepulcher today. I peered in every cranny, looked in every altar alcove. I was benumbed again with the numbers of icons, the candles and the sumptuous oil lamps. I had my fill of both priests and tourists, each pressing against the other in that place. Somewhere here, somewhere very near, Y'shua hung from that cross, suspended, alone, with even God removed from him.

Now I am sitting in one of the most beautiful places in all the city of Jerusalem, the Garden Tomb. I am sitting under a huge, gnarled pine tree, lavishing me with welcome shade on a very hot summer day. I'm encased in flowers. Not the flowers of a funeral parlor; these flowers are all living, magnificently tended. My ears are filled with the singing of birds. So many are they, and their voices so lush, the talking of tour groups is reduced to a hum. My little electronic typewriter is on my lap. And before me is the tomb many believe to be the place they laid the body of my Lord once he had died.

For myself, I'm a hold-out for the traditional site. But no one can sit down in there and do much thinking about the death Y'shua died. The Garden Tomb is a far better place to think, to pray, and to write.

But as near as I have been geographically today to the place of his death, his burial, and his resurrection, I am closer to *him* in the words of the poem he sang. Psalm 22 draws me nearer to him than does the Garden Tomb or the Holy Sepulcher. For the psalm is indisputable, its relation to his dying unquestioned.

Though I walked today very near the place where Jesus walked and suffered and died, as I turn again to the words of Psalm 22, I know that I am there *exactly*. Let's turn there now.

## The Structure of Pain

For us to appreciate the psalm of our Savior's passion, it is helpful to grasp the pattern of the psalms of individual lament. These psalms, frequent in the Bible, have a distinct pattern with several elements in more or less regular appearance:

- an opening cry to God for help
- a statement of lament, using three pronouns:

> I am hurting!
> *You* [God] don't care!
> *They* [the enemy] are winning!

- a confession of trust, in which the psalmist states his deep conviction of the reality of Yahweh in his life
- the presentation of petition, using three verbs:

> *Hear* me! (Relates to the pronoun *you*)
> *Save* me! (Relates to the pronoun I)
> *Punish* them! (Relates to the pronoun *they*)

- motivations to God to respond to his prayer, *or* a conviction of being heard.
- a vow to praise Yahweh when the prayer has been answered, *or* praise given to God because he has already responded.
- sometimes the praise will be followed by a section of instruction to the congregation

This is the pattern of Psalm 22, the psalm of the cross. As we enter the poem, we will see these various elements interplay against each other.

**The Singers of the Psalm**

When we come to this psalm, we also need to have in mind the varied singers of this poem. While the ultimate singer is Y'shua, the psalm was first the song of David and the song of the community. This means that the poem needs to be read on different levels:

- The poem was first a psalm of David, in which he expressed his genuine complaint against God in a time of particular anguish.
- The poem then became a part of the hymnody of Israel in the temple worship. Many people who sang this poem, then and now, feel the emotions of these words strongly.
- Ultimately and essentially, the poem is the libretto for the passion of the Savior. The words are distinctly the words of Y'shua.

These three levels of meaning are not like the levels of meaning that medieval scholars foisted upon the text of the Bible. These are levels of meaning that the text itself demands.

- The heading tells us this was a psalm of David.
- The heading also states that it was given to the director of music to be used in the temple worship; hence, it would be sung by many people.
- We know that the psalm was sung by Y'shua.

With the structure and the singers in mind, we may now hear the opening words of Psalm 22.

## God So Far Away

Psalm 22 begins with the cry that God is so very distant at a time when the psalmist needs him the most. These were first the words of David in his distress. They have been sung by many hurting people through the ages. But none sang them so deeply as did Y'shua that day on the cross:

> My God, my God, why have you forsaken me?
>     Why are you so far from saving me,
>     so far from the words of my groaning?
> O my God, I cry out by day, but you do not an-
> swer,
>     by night, and am not silent (Psalm 22:1-2).

These words contain the opening cry, "My God," and the initial words of the lament that the pattern presents. In these verses the psalmist emphasizes the distancing of God from him during the time of his own ceaseless prayer for nearness.

## Lament and Faith

Sometimes Christians are made to think they will never really have periods of doubt or distress. They are told that if they do have times like these, it is due to some inadequacy on their part. It is because they are not really spiritual. Perhaps they are not sufficiently under the control of the Holy Spirit. Perhaps it is because of some unconfessed sin.

Such Christians who do hurt and who are told that they must not hurt may crack up. They may find the pressures of their own pain and the denial of that pain by others to be an unendurable tension. Sometimes such Christians wind up taking their lives rather than facing their troubles.

What a shame that is!

But it happens. A close friend of mine took his own life just a few weeks ago. We do not know all the reasons, of course. It may be that he was that kind of person who believed that he shouldn't have the distresses he was having.

Since he was unable to talk to anyone fully about it, he wound up taking his life.

One well-known writer on biblical themes says he does not like the psalms because they betray people in distress, which is unbecoming to their faith. He says these passages are a mark of an inadequate work of the Holy Spirit in their lives.

But the fact is this: *Believers do hurt sometimes.*

Some believers may hurt very much indeed!

Perhaps their hurt is occasioned by sin,

perhaps by weakness of faith,

perhaps by not yielding to the Spirit.

Perhaps.

But not always!

Sometimes there may be no weakness or lack of faith at all. It may be that in their case God has allowed them to go through an extraordinarily difficult situation for reasons that are hidden in the mystery of his own consummate glory.

What a hurting believer needs is not to be told that a real, Spirit-filled Christian does not hurt. A hurting believer needs someone to come alongside and say, "I too have hurt. Here is how God has helped me in my distress."

## The Scream of Y'shua

Before anyone dismisses the psalms too quickly on the basis of a supposed superior spirituality, let him or her think again of the words of this poem on the lips of the Savior Y'shua.

Do you still see him?

There he hangs.

Suspended.

Alone.

And God is gone.

God was gone for him that day. Heaven was silent, the sky was dark, *and God was gone!*

God gone! The words seem not to compute.

God is never gone. He promises never to leave or to forsake his people. God is near, nearer than a brother. God makes promises to his people that the trials they face will never be stronger than they can bear. There will always be an escape. They will be able to bear it. God cares!

Yet for Y'shua on that dark afternoon, there was an unnatural stillness in the Jerusalem air. God was gone!

And there are times when this is exactly what we feel, too.

All of the promises of the Bible notwithstanding—there may be times in the believer's life when it really seems that God *is* gone.

This is what Y'shua felt in his humanity. And in his human scream to a distant God, Y'shua shows us he understands the worst fears of the human heart.

The scream of Y'shua had another edge to it, however. We have already anticipated this. Because of what he had become, as he became sin for us, there was more than just the human feeling that God was distant.

For Y'shua there was another dimension. A dimension so fraught with mystery, so tied to things we do not understand, that we may only ask a question. Is it possible that in some manner there was some fracturing of the relationship between the Father and the Son that day? Is it possible that the eternal unity of the godhead was somehow in danger? Because the Son had become sin, did the Father really turn completely away from him, if only for a moment?

These are questions I suspect we cannot answer. Even to raise them is to chance misspeaking, to risk theological error, to misrepresent God.

But something happened that day. Something so terrible that Y'shua had to sing the song of Passion. He screamed out the words of this psalm, not in Hebrew, but in Aramaic.

"O my God," he said.

"O my God!"

"Why?" he said.

"Why have you forsaken *me*?"

## Y'shua's Faith

The psalms of lament provide not only the deepest expressions of human pain, they also provide the strongest assertions of resolute faith. For the same person may say both things in the same context! In fact, this is the genuine marvel of these psalms.

When a believer is hurting, that person is still a *believer*. The one who screams to God still believes in God. That is why the prayer is addressed to *him*!

For this reason we find in these poems an interplay of lament and confession, a moving from despair to hope, from pain to trust.

David gave Y'shua these words of trust:

> But you are holy;
>     the one enthroned on the praises of Israel!
> In you our fathers trusted,
>     they trusted, and you delivered them.
> They cried out to you and were saved,
>     in you they trusted, and they were not
>     ashamed!

(Psalm 22:3-5, personal translation).

In these words, Y'shua asserted his basis for continuing trust in his Father. Yahweh is the holy one. There is none like him. He is distinct, removed, awesome, and grand. But he has made the praises of his people the place of his dwelling. It is as though the praises of Israel have risen up to him and have become the cushion for his throne.

Moreover, Y'shua in his humanity was a part of the continuing people of faith. From Abraham and Sarah onward there have always been men and women of faith who have prayed to God in times of deep distress. God has been faithful to the family of Abraham, Isaac, and Jacob. Since he has been faithful to the fathers and their descendants, a hurting believer may take confidence in his own situation for that same faithfulness.

**New Pain**

Psalm 22 is a marvelous text. It describes so well how a person who is hurting really feels. It moves back and forth between hurt and trust. This is because the hurting believer is still trusting, but in trust is still hurting. This is so much the way we are.

And it is how *he* was that day. He was trusting and he was hurting; he was doing both together.

The pain of his suffering was dehumanizing. At one point he screamed out, "I am a worm and not a man!" (Psalm 22:6). The prophet Isaiah described the same dehumanizing phenomenon in the suffering of the Servant:

> his appearance was so disfigured
>> beyond that of any man
> and his form marred beyond human likeness
>> (Isaiah 52:14).

The words of the Passion psalm gave our Savior vent to the pain of the night and the torment of the day. All of the mocking he had endured, all the jibes and taunts, all the nastiness and vileness of his tormentors caused him to say:

> But I am a worm and not a man,
>> scorned by men and despised by the people.
> All who see me mock me;
>> they hurl insults, shaking their heads:

> "He trusts in the LORD;
>> let the LORD rescue him.
> Let him deliver him,
>> since he delights in him"
>> (Psalm 22:6-8)

### New Faith

From this new lament, which expresses the "they" (the enemies) element, our Lord was given words by this psalm to express anew his confidence in Yahweh. Earlier he had spoken of the history of his people (verses 3-5). Now he speaks of his own experience in his humanity in the trust of Yahweh:

> Yet you brought me out of the womb;
>> you made me trust in you
>> even at my mother's breast.

From birth I was cast upon you;
> from my mother's womb you have been my
God
> (Psalm 22:9-10).

In these words, Y'shua affirmed the life-long relationship he had with the Father. It began with his birth and continued from that moment. He learned it from his mother.

These words affirm as well the central role a mother has in the nurture of her child's developing faith in God. There is nothing so helpless as a baby. For that child there is nothing so comforting as the arms and breasts of its mother. There is a real sense in which we may say that we first learn to trust in God when we are held in our mother's arms.

For the baby Y'shua, that mother was Mary, the woman we are instructed to call "blessed" (Luke 1:48). How fitting that he would speak of learning faith from his mother, when she was there, at the foot of the cross, with the other women and with John.

## Come Near!

It is in this setting of faith in the midst of despair, of confidence in the midst of lament, that the Savior was given words to pray to Yahweh to come near:

> Do not be far from me,
>> for trouble is near
>> and there is no one to help (Psalm 22:11).

Remember the pattern? After the lament and the confession we expect to see the petition. This usually has three types of verbs: hear, save, punish. This psalm focuses on the first two. The imperative he makes to his Father is in the "hear" category. He believes he is alone. God must come near. God must take notice. Y'shua cannot bear it alone.

He will repeat this imperative: "But you, O Yahweh, be not far off!" (verse 19). The whole psalm turns on the distancing and nearness of God.

## On the Cross

Crucifixion was a Roman form of execution. It was unknown among the Hebrews in the time of David. The patterns of execution in Old Testament days were by stoning and by bow and arrow. People simply were not put to death by crucifixion (although on occasion the corpse of an enemy might be impaled).

The language of David in the central part of Psalm 22 is simply stunning. He used hyperbole to accentuate his own suffering. He does not tell us what the trouble was; he lets his impassioned language build word pictures for us.

At one point David uses a most unexpected wording: He says that his enemies pierced his hands and his feet (Psalm 22:16). The Hebrew verb he uses is problematic. And well it might be. There simply was no such practice in his day. Yet the Jewish translators of the Bible into Greek understood the meaning of the word, even if they were as surprised by it as are we.

As the text stands now in the Hebrew Bible, we have a most unconvincing phrase: "as the lion, my hands and my feet." This translation is an expedient for a difficulty. It simply does not fit the rest of the text. David describes his enemies in animal terms. They are like bulls and lions (verses 12-13, 21), like dogs and wild oxen (verses 20-21). David is not the lion in this text; the enemies are like lions.

The Spirit of God has given David leave to describe the sufferings of the Savior in language that was not a part of his own experience. This is like his wording in Psalm 110; in this text he is David the Prophet (see Matthew 22:43).

Note the descriptive phrases David uses in his prophetic libretto for the death of the Savior:

> I am poured out like water,
>    and all my bones are out of joint.
> My heart has turned to wax;
>    it has melted away within me.
> My strength is dried up like a potsherd,
>    and my tongue sticks to the roof of my mouth
>       (Psalm 22:14-15).

These words describe his intense physical suffering as he was dying on the cross. His body was thrust forward at an unnatural position, causing organs to press strongly against each other. He is greatly dehydrated. The weight of his body is pulling his bones out of joint. His heart barely functions. These poetic words might have been written by an eyewitness. In some ways they were. David saw these things in his mind's eye as he described his own hurt in vivid language of the imagination.

**The Dogs Below**

In another section of the intense lament, David gives our Lord these words for his song of the cross:

> Dogs have surrounded me;
>> a band of evil men has encircled me,
>> they have pierced my hands and my feet.
> I can count all my bones;
>> people stare and gloat over me.
> They divide my garments among them
>> and cast lots for my clothing
>>> (Psalm 22:16-18).

It's uncanny, isn't it? David lived a thousand years before the Savior died his cruel death. Yet the language he used to describe his own suffering became the explicit description of the Savior's death.

- There are the Roman soldiers who have pierced his wrists and his feet; now they are gambling for his garment (Luke 23:34; John 19:23-24).
- There are enemies all about him, heaping cursings on him (Mark 15:29-32).
- And there were his bones, pressing out from unnatural pressure as he hangs there dying.

**Once More He Screams**

With the dogs below and no God near, once more Y'shua screams for help. Once more he asks Yahweh to come near. Now he screams for deliverance:

> But you, O LORD, be not far off;
>> O my Strength, come quickly to help me.
> Deliver my life from the sword,
>> my precious life from the power of the dogs.

Rescue me from the mouth of the lions;
　　save me from the horns of the wild oxen.
　　(Psalm 22:19-21).

The petition is complete. He has expressed both his pain and his hope. Now it is up to God to act. For the psalmist there remains the vow to praise God and the anticipation that he will answer his prayer. We will turn to these issues in our next chapter.

**Not Alone**

What transpired that day when Y'shua, God's Son, was on that cross can never fully be known. But a great deal of what happened that day is told to us in the Bible.

- The gospels describe the events of that day.
- The epistles explain the meaning of that day.
- The prophets foretell the importance of that day.

But it is the psalms that let us know something of what Y'shua thought, how he suffered, what he prayed, the words of music that choked within the dryness of his throat.

The most wonderful thing about the psalm of Passion is that it does not end in death.

The psalm leads on to victory.

*Y'shua was not alone!*

Yahweh was near!

This song that began with such a lament becomes one of the most glorious hymns of praise of all.

Y'shua sings another day!

CHAPTER

# 9

## Resurrection Song

**T**he hours pass so slowly.
There he hangs.
Suspended.
But *he is no longer alone*
Yahweh is there!
And he knows his presence.
And he senses his victory.

### The Rest of the Song

I suspect that many Christians have a sense that the death of the Lord Jesus Christ was predicted by the Old Testament prophets. They would point to Isaiah 53 and Psalm 22 as the major passages making this prediction.

But it is not as commonly known that the Old Testament texts speak as strongly of his resurrection as they do of his dying. Yet this is precisely the teaching of our Lord and of the apostles.

Think back again to the words of the resurrected Y'shua to the disciples on the road to Emmaus. Remember how he said to them,

> How foolish you are, and how slow of heart to believe all that the prophets have spoken! Did not the Messiah have to suffer these things and then enter his glory? (Luke 24:26).

Then, later, he spoke to the rest of the disciples in Jerusalem and spoke these startling words:

> This is what is written: The Messiah will suffer
> and rise from the dead on the third day, and re-
> pentance and forgiveness of sins will be
> preached in his name to all nations, beginning
> at Jerusalem (Luke 24:46-47).

Similarly, the apostle Paul defined the essence of the gospel as made of two facts: (1) that Messiah died for our sins, and (2) that he was raised on the third day (1 Corinthians 15:3-5). Both of these great truths were predicted in the Scriptures and were validated in the lives of the disciples.

This means the rest of the story, the rest of the song, must be in the Hebrew Bible. It was not "Plan B" to raise Y'shua from the grave. It was God's intention from the beginning. It was always part of the music.

So let's go back to the Song of Passion, Psalm 22, and hear the rest of the song. Y'shua says we can find it if we are not foolish and slow of heart to believe. As we go back to hear the rest of the music, however, we may need to have a fresh sense of the meaning and wonder of the name of God. The psalm makes sense only in this way.

### Yahweh Hears

The name of God in the Hebrew Bible is *Yahweh*, a word I have used repeatedly in this study. It is a strange irony that many Christian people do not know the name of God in the Bible. We know the word "Jehovah," but are not aware that this word is a conflation of two different words for God's name. While it has gained acceptance through centuries of use, it is not really the Hebrew word that expresses the name of God. That name is *Yahweh*.

God revealed the meaning and significance of his name to his great servant Moses in the early chapters of the book of Exodus.

Do you recall the scene? Moses was in the back side of the desert, a fugitive from Egypt because of a rash act in killing an Egyptian taskmaster. He lived forty years tending sheep and goats, rearing a family, and perhaps having no hope of ever being with his people again in this life.

During this period the lot of his people had become extremely difficult. The ruinous policies of oppression that began before Moses' birth were growing ever more severe. The people screamed out to God above for help, for salvation, for release from the heavy burden of their servitude.

In that situation, God revealed the meaning of his name as the prelude to the revelation of his salvation. The text says:

> God heard their groaning and he remembered his covenant with Abraham, with Isaac and with Jacob. So God looked on the Israelites and was concerned about them (Exodus 2:24-25).

There are four verbs in these verses that describe the action of God. We may put these verbs in the present tense to stress them more fully:

- God hears!
- God remembers!
- God sees!
- God knows!

In these Hebrew verbs we find the essence of the character of God revealed more fully to Moses in the interchange at the burning bush (Exodus 3:1-15).

There Moses learns that God has a name that characterizes his relationship with his people. When God's people are hurting, he is not unaware; he feels the hurt of his people because he is tied to them by his compelling covenant bond. He hears! He remembers! He sees! He knows!

Moreover, he comes down to deliver! And he promises to be with his people. The name of God is a name of active relationship, assuring the bright destiny of his people.

Now think of Y'shua on the cross. Hanging there. Suspended. Believing he is all alone.

Would not Yahweh the father hear him as he heard the voice of his people long ago? Would not Yahweh the father remember him as he remembered his covenant with his people long ago? Would not Yahweh his father see him as he saw his people long ago? Would not Yahweh the father of mercies know with concern?

The song must have another verse!
*Yahweh hears!*

## Yahweh Hears Y'shua

Among the happiest words in all hymnody are these words of confidence that David gave to Y'shua to express his faith while still suspended on the cross: God was near! He had heard! He would deliver him!

> For he has not despised or disdained
>> the suffering of the afflicted one;
> he has not hidden his face from him
>> but *has listened* to his cry for help (Psalm 22:24).

After all the suffering our Lord went through, after all the pain, then he knew again the presence of God. Even on the cross he knew that presence. For it is only on the cross that these words have meaning.

The pattern of the psalm of lament never served man better than it served Y'shua on that long, awful afternoon. The lament pattern, you remember, begins with a cry for help. It then proceeds with the lament proper, with the use of three pronouns: I am hurting, *You* (God) do not care, and *They* (the enemy) are winning. In this lament the psalmist expresses the depths of his pain and crisis of faith.

The lament then turns to confession of trust in God. From the same person come words of anger and resentment as well as hope and peace. This is the way we are when we are hurting and when we still believe in God!

Then the psalmist expresses his petition: Hear me! Save me! Punish them! These strong imperatives relate directly to the pronouns of the lament. Then comes the plea for God to hear or the statement that God has already heard. In Psalm 22 it is the latter that happens. Yahweh has heard Y'shua. The Savior is not alone.

## Y'shua the Afflicted

Y'shua identified with the hurting people of the earth. One psalm we have looked at earlier in this study ends with these words:

Yet I am poor and needy;
    may the Lord think of me.
You are my help and my deliverer;
    O my God, do not delay
        (Psalm 40:17).

Such were the words of Y'shua about himself. Now make no mistake here! It is not that he suffered from a poor sense of self-esteem, concerning which so much is made today. No one who has read the gospel narrative would say that about him!

The point is this: He identified with the hurting of this world, that in sharing their hurt he might deliver us all from pain.

Remember how Isaiah puts it?

He grew up before him like a tender shoot,
    and like a root out of dry ground.
He had no beauty or majesty to attract us to him,
    nothing in his appearance that we should
        desire him.

He was despised and rejected by men,
    a man of sorrows, and familiar with suffering.
Like one from whom men hide their faces
    he was despised, and we esteemed him not
        (Isaiah 53:2-3).

It was preeminently when the Savior was on the cross that he was needy. It was there that he was "the afflicted one" (Psalm 22:24). It was especially there that he was "a man of sorrows, familiar with suffering" (Isaiah 53:3).

It was on the cross that he cried out to his God for notice, for nearness, for help. The words of Psalm 40:17 certainly apply:

"You are my help and my deliverer;
    O my God, do not delay."

Then God came near.
    Then Yahweh stooped down.
        Then his Father reached out his hand.
And Y'shua's song of lament became a song of praise.

## Y'shua's Praise

With the confidence that Yahweh was near, Y'shua was able to make this vow of praise:

> I will declare your name to my brothers;
>> in the congregation I will praise you.
>>> (Psalm 22:22).

That is, there on the cross Jesus could say he would live again and that he would show himself alive to his friends and would give praise to God.

He *knew* he would live again.

Even on the cross, he *knew*!

As his blood dripped from his wounds, tracked paths down the rough wood of the cross, made small puddles there in the rocky sand—he *knew* he would live again!

He was still hanging there. Still suspended. But no longer alone. Even as his strength was sagging, there was hope of a new song that he would sing with his friends. He *knew* .

Hence, his call for praise to God comes in the context of covenant solidarity. He calls for all descendants of the fathers of promise to join him in praise of God:

> You who fear the LORD, praise him!
>> All you descendants of Jacob, honor him!
>> Revere him, all you descendants of Israel!
>>> (Psalm 22:23).

The deliverance of Y'shua from the bonds of death is part of the continuing work of Yahweh in keeping covenant faith with his people. Y'shua came as the Messiah of Israel. The first call to praise Yahweh appropriately goes to the Jewish people, the descendants of Jacob/Israel.

Moreover, Y'shua's words of praise, bequeathed to him by the poet David, include a special invitation to the poor and the disenfranchised, those with whom he had made such a close identification:

> The poor will eat and be satisfied;
>> they who seek the LORD will praise him—
>> may your hearts live forever!
>>> (Psalm 22:26).

But as for himself, there is the strong vow of praise. He will praise Yahweh in the midst of the great congregation. His vows will be paid:

> From you comes my praise in the great assembly;
>> before those who fear you will I fulfill my vows.
> (Psalm 22:25).

This is precisely what he did.

On the road to Emmaus and then again that evening in Jerusalem, Jesus showed himself before his friends to keep his vows of praise to Yahweh. On each occasion that the risen Lord showed himself alive, it was in fulfillment of his vow.

He appeared to individuals such as Mary of Magdala and Peter, and later to Paul. He appeared to groups of women and men. He appeared to his disciples. At one point he appeared to a group of over five hundred. In each of these appearances he demonstrated what Yahweh had done. In each he showed that God had heard his cry. In each he magnified the Father.

Psalm 22 presents not only the words of Y'shua's pain as he was suspended on the cross; the poem also gives his vow of praise to the Father for the prospect of his resurrection.

When he screamed from the cross the first words of Psalm 22 (Matthew 27:46), all of the poem lay before him. All that long afternoon these words worked their wonder in him. All that afternoon he dealt first with his grief and then turned to hope. All that afternoon Psalm 22 was *his* song.

Indeed, Y'shua is *Lord of Song*!

## The Gospel of Y'shua

The vow of Y'shua on the cross was that he would praise his father for the deliverance he was about to receive. A part of that vow extended directly to his friends, for it was to them that he would show himself first.

The vow of Y'shua extended then to the whole Jewish community. For he had come as the Messiah of Israel in God's fulfillment of covenant promise. Certainly the word would go first to the people of Israel, the descendants of Jacob (Psalm 22:23).

But Y'shua had come to redeem all mankind. The purpose of the Jewish Messiah was not just to deliver Jewish people. God's intention in his promised one was always for the peoples of all races and all ethnic groups.

This was the promise of God from the beginning. When Yahweh first spoke to Abram and brought him into covenant relationship with himself, it was with the final intention to bring the blessing of Abram's seed to all families of the earth (Genesis 12:3).

For these reasons, we find the words of Y'shua in Psalm 22:27-28 to be his promise of the spread of the gospel to the ends of the earth:

> All the ends of the earth
>     will remember and turn to the LORD,
> and all the families of the nations
>     will bow down before him,
> for dominion belongs to the LORD
>     and he rules over the nations.

It was quite possibly just this passage that the risen Y'shua had in mind when he said that the Old Testament Scriptures contained the message that "repentance and forgiveness of sins will be preached in his name to all nations, beginning at Jerusalem" (Luke 24:47). This text includes all peoples and families. It calls for all to come to the knowledge of the Great King, Yahweh, and to the great Y'shua whom the father has delivered from death itself.

The spreading of the gospel of Y'shua to all nations was an essential part of the plan of God from the beginning. World mission is not an innovation of modern times; it is a biblical priority from the beginning. And world mission was always a central demand issuing out of the resurrection of Y'shua.

### The Preaching of the Resurrection

The disciples to whom Y'shua showed himself must have been exquisitely joyful. He had turned their night into day, their death into life. Now he was there! Now life was new.

When the empowering of the Holy Spirit had come, the disciples were renewed inwardly to proclaim the message of the resurrection of Y'shua with a boldness and a daring that came only from God.

Never again would they be chided for being slow of heart or foolish when it came to seeing the evidences of the gospel story in the Scriptures of their people.

Peter's preaching on Pentecost is the sterling example of the lessons these believers in Y'shua had learned. The report of his sermon is necessarily abbreviated. But the text we read is permeated with citations from the Hebrew Bible. Peter had learned that the details of the life, death, and resurrection of Y'shua were taught in the Scriptures fully and adequately.

For this reason, when Peter wanted to demonstrate that the Hebrew Bible spoke of the Messiah's resurrection, he used a psalm of David. He spoke of how Y'shua died, then said that it was absolutely necessary for God to raise Y'shua from the dead. "It was impossible for death to keep its hold on him" (Acts 2:24). Then he turned to the six-teenth psalm and said these words were sung by David about Y'shua:

> I have set the Lord always before me.
> Because he is at my right hand,
> I will not be shaken.
> Therefore my heart is glad and my tongue re-joices;
> my body also will live in hope,
> because you will not abandon me to the grave,
> nor will you let your Holy One see decay.
> You have made known to me the path of life;
> you will fill me with joy in your presence.

Peter quoted these words from Psalm 16:8-11 and then said they were words that David, as prophet, had spoken specifically about Y'shua. Peter's argument ran this way: If David meant these words about himself, then why was he

not physically present with them, instead of being com-
memorated by a tomb in Jerusalem very near where they
were standing? Since David was obviously dead and
buried, these words must relate to another; it is to Y'shua
they belong!

Peter says: "Seeing what was ahead, he [David] spoke
of the resurrection of the Messiah, that he was not aban-
doned to the grave, nor did his body see decay" (Acts 2:31).
Y'shua was resurrected by the Father; all present were witnesses. And now, Peter declared, the risen Y'shua was present with the Father and had now sent the outpouring of the
Holy Spirit which had so amazed the crowd of Jewish on-
lookers.

The preaching of the resurrection in the early church
was based upon eyewitness accounts of the miracle, and
the scriptural validation of God's predetermined decision
to raise his Son from the dead.

A significant part of that scriptural validation is in the
psalms, for they form the libretto of the passion and the
victory songs of celebration: Y'shua will live again.

## The Celebration

It seems to me wonderfully fitting that the psalm of
passion that began with such a desperate call for help ends
in a perpetual celebration.

The psalm projects the happiness of the people of God
in this life—and in the life to come—because of the things
he has done for the Singer of this psalm. The psalm also
declares the way in which the central story of God's deliverance will be told from one generation to another. This is
the wonderful spread of the gospel message of the resurrected Y'shua:

All the rich of the earth will feast and worship;
    all who go down to the dust will kneel before
him—
    those who cannot keep themselves alive.
Posterity will serve him;
    future generations will be told about the Lord.

They will proclaim his righteousness
   to a people yet unborn—
   for he has done it (Psalm 22:29-31).

In some ways, the last words of the psalm are the most important: "He *has done it!*" He *has* done it.

- Y'shua has died the death that brings us peace with God.
- The Father has raised Y'shua and has exalted him to a position of highest glory.

When Y'shua was about to die, he was able to say, "It is finished." He could say that because his death was then accomplished, and the hope of the resurrection was certain.

And we get to join his party! Whenever we tell someone of the death he died for them and the life he lives for them, we join the party of eternity, the celebration of the ages.

Who would have thought that a poem that begins as Psalm 22 does would end as this one does?

Who but God?

And who but Y'shua could sing it rightly?

*He is Lord of Song!*

# 10

# Triumph
# Song

**T**he songs of the Savior began with the song he sang in heaven. Just before he left his heavenly estate to become man, he sang to his Father, "I have come to do your pleasure." He who was ever God divested himself of the power and privileges of deity and placed himself, by the power of the Holy Spirit, into a fertilized egg in the womb of the woman God chose to be his human mother. There is no mystery so profound as the mystery of God becoming man.

Then he lived his life so fully by the power of the Holy Spirit that he entirely fulfilled the demands of the Torah of Yahweh. At last there was one who was able to live fully and rightly before God! He taught, he preached, he led, and he served. In all of his life he glorified the father and pointed men and women to him.

Then Y'shua died. His death was the centerpiece of all history. In his death he reconciled God and man. In his death, he the righteous became sin, that all who are sinners might become righteous before God. And while he was dying, even as he had lived, there were words to sing from the hymnal of Israel. For in his life and in his death, Y'shua was Lord of Song.

Though he died, he did not remain captive to death. Death could not hold him. The power of God that had created the universe, that had brought Israel out of slavery, that delivered men and women from innumerable troubles—that power in its fullness burst him forth from death to life on that first Easter morning.

All of these events were part of the song that he sang. For even on the cross there were words for him to sing from the Passion Libretto that presented the solid hope of his victory. For the joy that was set before him, he was enabled by the Spirit of God to endure the cross and all its pain. Even then he knew what lay ahead for him.

But there is another song to sing. It is the song of final triumph over the evil that still lies in mankind. There is still ahead the victory song when the slain and risen Lamb of God returns to earth as the conquering hero, King of kings, Lord of lords, with glory for ever.

## The Road to Jerusalem

King David wrote the song for our Lord's triumphal entry into the Holy City of Jerusalem. David wrote this song in one of the greatest and most difficult moments of his life. The song was aborning during the journey of the holy Ark back to Jerusalem. This is a story of drama and pathos. It is an extraordinary story of the holiness of Yahweh. It is a story of partial fulfillment and infinite longing, of painful frustration and abiding hope. It is the story of the road to Jerusalem.

## The Loss of the Holy Ark

It is difficult for the modern reader, even for one sympathetic with the theology of the Hebrew Bible, to appreciate fully the calamity Israel suffered when she lost the holy Ark.

Perhaps you remember the story. It happened way back in the period of the judges. The tribes of Israel, not yet consolidated into a nation, were in perpetual struggle with enemy nations. Their nemesis was Philistia, the warlike people who had settled the coastlands of Palestine. As the people of Israel were building their positions in the highlands and the lower hills, the Philistines were becoming entrenched on the coast. They were now a potent rival for all of the land with the tribes of Israel.

The definitive battle came during the early adulthood of the judge and prophet Samuel. The armies of Israel were encamped at Ebenezer, and the armies of Philistia were at Aphek (near modern Tel Aviv).

The early confrontations of the battle went poorly for Israel. They lost thousands of men; they were frightfully demoralized. They began to curse the Lord for having brought them to such a sorry state.

Then they thought of their ace in the hole. They sent back to Shiloh, where the center of the worship of Yahweh had been established, and they had the holy Ark brought to their camp. When they had the Ark in the center of their camp, they believed they were invincible. Had not Moses led their fathers against innumerable foes by the power of the Ark? Had not Joshua led their parents in victory after victory with the presence of the Ark?

They shouted so very loud when the Ark arrived that they sent the armies of Philistia into hysteria. Soldiers in the enemy camp tried to stave off one another's fear by encouraging each other at least to die like men.

The narrator of the battle is especially terse as he describes the battle scene the next day. Here on one side are the pagan armies of Philistia, their feathered finery worn in mock bravado for the sure defeat they faced. On the other side are the confident armies of Israel, soldiers already planning how they will spend their leaves with the women of the cities they were about to defeat. This is what the narrator says happened:

> So the Philistines fought, and the Israelites were defeated and every man fled to his tent. The slaughter was very great; Israel lost thirty thousand foot soldiers. The ark of God was captured, and Eli's two sons, Hophni and Phinehas, died (1 Samuel 4:10-11).

What a surprise! Battle lost, priests dead, Ark gone! This was such a calamity that when the news came to the aged priest Eli, he fell off his chair onto his back, broke his neck, and died. The pregnant wife of Phinehas, one of Eli's sons who perished, went into premature labor. She died as a son was born. The sad midwives named the son

"Ichabod," a chilling name aptly describing the horrors of the day: "No glory." For the glory of Yahweh had departed. Battle lost, priests dead, Ark gone!

## No Magic Box

What had happened, of course, is that the armies of Israel had treated the holy Ark as a magic box. It wasn't. Their calamity came because they had forgotten the holiness of Yahweh and the holiness of the special box that represented his presence in their midst.

The holy Ark was a mark of the presence of Yahweh. It was a box, but not a magic box. It had been made of acacia wood and measured approximately three feet long, one and one-half feet wide, and two and one-quarter feet high. It was overlaid with pure gold. There were rings at the corners to hold poles for carrying the ark. There were special golden implements that went into the Ark. Along with these were several symbols of the power of God amidst his people: a sample of the bread of the Presence, the second set of stone tablets with the Ten Words from Mount Sinai, a pot of manna, and Aaron's rod that budded. Over the box was the mercy seat, bedecked with cherubim. This box of mystery was the potent symbol of the presence of the Lord of the universe in the encampments of his people.

It was not to be treated as a magic box. The error of the armies of Israel—and the error of modern Hollywood in the popular film *Raiders of the Lost Ark*—is to think of the box as a magical device one may use to enforce one's will.

The Ark was gone, and with it went the vital force of the presence of Yahweh among his people.

## No Prize

The Ark was also no prize to the Philistines. Wherever they tried to put it havoc ensued. They set it up first in a temple to their god Dagon in Ashdod. This was to symbolize the victory of Dagon over Yahweh . . . so they supposed.

The next morning the image of Dagon was on its face before the Ark. They righted their idol. But the next morning things were worse. It was on its face again, this time with head and hands broken off. Meanwhile, the community suffered an epidemic of grievously painful tumors. The good people of Ashdod promptly had enough of the Ark; they sent it on its way to Gath. Plague broke out in Gath as well. The citizens of Gath forwarded the Ark to Ekron. What the armies of Israel had been unable to do, the Ark of God brought about: the routing of the enemy in his own principal cities.

Finally they sent it back to Israel. The Ark was placed on a cart along with golden images of the tumors and the rats that were associated with the plague. Two cows that had calved were hitched to the cart. With their udders full and their maternal instincts frightfully confused, the cows went away from their calves, lowing all the way to Beth Shemesh.

There the Ark was received back by the people of Israel with great sacrifices and rejoicing. The Ark was placed in a farmer's field, and the Philistine rulers who watched from a distance were glad to be rid of the box.

**The Holy Ark**

The story of bringing the Ark back to Israel ends on as sad a note as it began. Some of the men of Beth Shemesh looked inside the ark when it arrived on the cart—a not unnatural thing to do.

But the Ark was holy.

Indescribably holy.

A symbol of the holiness of Yahweh.

Because of their curiosity, some seventy men lost their lives. For one curious look, God struck them dead! The people's response was quite understandable. They asked, "Who can stand in the presence of the LORD, this holy God?" (1 Samuel 6:20). They were as dismayed as the Philistines had been. Like the Philistines, they wanted the Ark to go elsewhere.

The Ark was moved by the men of Kiriath Jearim to the home of Abinadab. And there it stayed. Twenty years passed. Then the godly Samuel led the people in a spiritual revival and in a military victory over the Philistines. Yahweh fought for them as of old, thundering from heaven, routing their foes. Samuel took a great stone and set it up as a memorial of that great victory. He named the stone *Ebenezer*, "stone of help," saying, "Thus far has the LORD helped us" (1 Samuel 7:12).

The Philistines were subdued; the Ark was at rest.

Years pass.

Saul's reign begins and ends.

David's reign begins and flourishes.

Still the holy Ark was in a farmer's field at Kiriath Jearim.

Then David captures the city of Jerusalem from the Jebusites who had taken it back since the initial conquest by Israel during the time of Joshua. In addition, David completed the conquest of the Philistines, bringing to an end their long threat against the security of Israel.

It was time to move the Ark!

## The Tale of Uzzah

When it came to the worship of God, David did not do things by halves. He sought to bring the Ark to the new capital of Jerusalem, and he wanted to do it in style.

David took thirty thousand men with him when he went to get the Ark of God. He set it on a new cart and then led in worship of Holy God with all of his might. The singers were in seven choirs; the instrumentalists used every instrument in the band. They were singing and dancing with great joy—the Ark was on its way to the new capital. What a day this was!

The path took a turn, an ox stumbled a bit, the Ark tottered, a godly man reached out his hand to steady the box . . . and God struck him dead!

The anger of Yahweh flashed down against Uzzah for his precipitous act. All he had done was to reach out to steady the tottering box. And God struck him dead!

The day that began with such joy ended with questions, doubt, and awful fear. As Yahweh had been angry with Uzzah, so David was angry with the Lord. In his fear and doubt, David breathed the sad words, "How can the ark of the LORD ever come to me?" (2 Samuel 6:9).

They took the Ark to the home of Obed-Edom the Gittite, where it stayed for three months. During that time, the household of that farmer was blessed by the presence of the box, the potent symbol of the presence of Yahweh.

## The Ark Comes to Jerusalem

David tried again. This time the instructions of Moses were followed to the letter: Men carried the Ark by poles inserted into loops on its sides. This time things were done according to Torah.

There again were the seven choirs. There again innumerable musicians. There again dancers.

Those carrying the Ark had gone only six steps when David called for them to halt. He ordered sacrifices of bull and calf. Then David stripped to a linen ephod and danced before Yahweh with all of his might.

As thousands of people made their way to Jerusalem, there was no one more fervent in his worship of God than David. So enraptured was he that his wife Michal, Saul's daughter, was scandalized as she saw him from her upper window.

But finally the Ark was in the city. David ordered many sacrifices to Yahweh and a great feast for the people.

But the most serious question of all remained: Who may stand before the holy Ark? Who may come before holy God?

## David's Song of the Ark

This story gives the background for Psalm 24, a poem we may call the psalm of the Ark. In this psalm David asks the poignant question central to all theology:

> Who may ascend the hill of the LORD?
> Who may stand in his holy place?
> (Psalm 24:3).

Scholars differ considerably in their understanding of Psalm 24, but most agree on its intended setting. It is the tragic and dramatic story we have just surveyed of David's bringing the holy Ark to Jerusalem.

The Ark is mystery. It is just a box: highly decorated, but just a box.

Yet it was not just a box. It was the potent symbol of the

residing presence of Yahweh. The Ark was mystery. The Ark was wonder. The Ark was power. Who may stand before it?

In the wrong hands it led to devastation, judgment, terrible illness.

In curious hands it led to the stilling judgment of God.

Even in well-meaning but improper hands, it led to death.

*Who may stand before Yahweh?*

Once the Ark was in place in the temporary housing David had prepared for it, he wrote Psalm 24, asking the central question of how one may rightly approach an indescribably holy God.

## He Is Sovereign

Psalm 24 begins with an affirmation of the sovereignty of Yahweh:

> To Yahweh does the earth belong,
>> and all that fills it;
> the inhabited land,
>> and all who dwell in it.
>>> (Psalm 24:1, personal translation, and so
>>> throughout).

In all the events centering on the adventures of the Ark, the one undeniable factor is the sovereignty of Yahweh. He is in control:

- He will not be manipulated.
- He will not be compromised.
- He will not be trivialized.

These things are true whether the offending party is misinformed, ignorant, well-meaning, or whatever. All suffered when they abused the Ark: errant Israel, pagan Philistines, godly Hebrews.

The earth and everything in it, the land and all who live on it—are his! And he will do as he wills. God is free to be God, or God is not God. This is unpleasant, even unpalatable—but a necessary element in our view of God.

The psalmist gives the reason for the sovereignty of the Lord in the second verse of the poem:

> For he founded it over the seas,
> and over the rivers he established it.

This wording, which seems so very peculiar to modern taste, is built upon a common imagery in the ancient world. A recurring poetic idea concerning the power of God is to say he is stronger than the mighty waters (see Psalm 93:4), or that he has established limits for the seas (see Proverbs 8:29).

This concept presents the biblical response to the paganism of that day which presumed there was a conflict between various gods, leading to the ordering of the universe. The biblical view, of course, is that there is one God only, and his name is Yahweh. The supposed watery forces of evil are under his complete control.

Hence, for the poet to say that God has firmly established the earth over the seas and rivers is not to describe some mystical land floating on some nether waters; it is a highly poetic way to emphasize the reality of Yahweh's sovereignty. *God is in control.* He is free to be God.

So back to our question: Who may approach him?

## Who May Come Near?

With a very high and holy view of God, the question comes most naturally—Who may approach him? This was the question of the people of Beth Shemesh after God had struck down seventy men who presumed to look inside the holy Ark. They asked, "Who can stand in the presence of Yahweh, this holy God?" (1 Samuel 6:20). That was also the question of David after God struck down Uzzah: "How can the ark of the LORD ever come to me?" (2 Samuel 6:9). And it is the central question of this psalm:

> Who may ascend the mount of Yahweh?
> Who may stand in his holy place?
> (Psalm 24:3)

The question has two answers. One is provisional, the other ultimate. The provisional answer comes from God's grace in Torah.

God has made a pathway for sinful women and sinful

139

men to come before him. They may not come on the basis
of their own righteousness; but having become righteous
in him, they may come nonetheless.

Yet there are demands upon them, demands of moral
and ritual purity. The book of Leviticus, for example, was
given to Israel to make that way of access clear and sure:
God may be approached by those who come to him in the
way he made possible.

This is certainly one way to read the words of verses 4
and 5 of our psalm:

> He who has clean hands and pure heart,
>> who has not lifted up his being to an idol,
>>> and does not swear by that which is false.
> He receives blessing from Yahweh,
>> and righteousness from the God of his salva-
>> tion.

These words bring to mind the principal concerns for
biblical morality. Fidelity to the Ten Words—particularly
loyalty to Yahweh as only God—certainly is demanded.

The basic issues presented by Psalm 15 come to mind.
The type of person who may dwell on the holy hill of the
sanctuary of Yahweh is one:

- who has a blameless walk
- who is faithful in his speech
- who is honorable with his neighbor
- who has right values
- who keeps his word no matter what
- who never hurts the weak

In this list of positive virtues of Torah, Psalm 15 presents the model of the life of faith. Psalm 24 seems at first
to take a similar stance.

**Where Is He?**

But the surprising verse 6 of Psalm 24 shows that more
than ordinary piety is intended. Psalm 24 calls for ultimate
purity.

Psalm 24 is not Psalm 15. This psalm is not calling for
one who fits the standard catalog of relative piety. Psalm

24 looks for the real thing: one who can stand every test of fidelity to Yahweh. Here is a literal rendering of the difficult words of verse 6:

> This generation is seeking him,
>> they are seeking your face, O Jacob!
>>> /Selah.

Many difficulties come with this verse. The usual solution is to assume that it is God who is being sought. For that reason the NIV reads this verse in this way: "Such is the generation of those who seek him, who seek your face, O God of Jacob." But this translation is based primarily on secondary evidence rather than the principal Hebrew readings.

The strict reading of the Hebrew text of this verse suggests that God is not being sought in this verse, *but man.* That is, the question before us is, "who may stand before God?" Who indeed! What *man* in all of Jacob can say, "Here I am; I may stand before the Lord!"

**There Is None**
> No one answers.
>> No one steps forward.
>>> No one dares!
> Everyone remembers Uzzah.
>> All recall the fear of David.
>>> Who else wishes to presume?

At the people's lack of response, the heart of the people sags. Since there is none who may stand before the Lord, all are saddened.

There is a sense that even the city walls are affected:
The walls of the city seem to slump.
> The gates sag.
>> The doors buckle.

Why was the holy Ark brought inside Jerusalem if there is no one who may stand before it in full confidence and in great praise of God?
> And the years pass.
>> Centuries pass.
>>> And then one comes!

**There He Comes!**

Dorothy Purdy has described the entry of Y'shua into Jerusalem on Palm Sunday in a lovely manner. Here are her words:

I Wonder

As He rode in
    through the palm branches
    and hosannas
    on the lowly donkey
I wonder—
    even then
    did He see
    great white horses
    being groomed
    for the reentry?
"And the armies which were in heaven followed him upon white horses, clothed in fine linen, white and clean."
        -Revelation 19:14

There is one who comes. There is one who comes without fear. There is one who comes in the name of Yahweh. There is one whose coming was so soundly anticipated by the Lord and all of his holy angels that when he came he *had* to be praised. When some attempted to still that praise, he said that the rocks would have to shout aloud should the people stifle his praise.

There is one.

His name is Y'shua.

It is he who comes in the name of Yahweh.

He may stand and not fear.

He is able to meet every demand of the most holy God and receive blessing from the Father. As he comes, there is the smile of all heaven, the rejoicing of all the people of God.

**And He Comes Again**

And one day he shall come again.

What a day that shall be!

When he comes, it shall not be as before.

142

The next time it will be on the white charger, not the lowly donkey.

The next time it will be as the victor over all enemies.

The next time it will not be to face judgment, cruel death, and mocking derision.

Next time—God bless us all!—next time it will be to receive glory and power and honor and worth and praise. Next time!

Next time the words of the ending of Psalm 24 will be sung by angels and Israel, by the cherubim and the church. Next time he comes, these will be our words of liturgical interaction to his glory:

> Lift up your heads, O you gates!
> Be lifted up, O you ancient doors!
> That the King of Glory may come in!
>> *Who is this King of Glory?*
>> *Yahweh awesomely mighty,*
>> *Yahweh victorious in battle!*
> Lift up your heads, O you gates!
> Lift up, O you ancient doors!
> That the King of Glory may come in!
>> *Who is he, this King of Glory?*
>> *Yahweh of Hosts,*
>> *He is the King of Glory!*

/Selah

(Psalm 24:7-10)

## His Song

You see, Psalm 24 is the psalm of the Victory. After the Lord Jesus has returned to earth to establish his kingdom, this ancient prayer of King David will have been answered.

For a thousand years after David asked the question, no one stepped forward. Then on Palm Sunday there he came, Y'shua of Nazareth, riding on a donkey, receiving the praise of the crowd—praise which became an unintended call for his death. For when the crowd chanted "Hosanna," they were singing the words of Psalm 118:25, "O Yahweh, save us!" That was precisely what he had come to do.

Two thousand years have passed. There is a sense in

143

which the gates still slump, the walls still sag. But one day he will come. And they will lift their heads!

## His Walls, His Gates

I sit outside the wall, at the base of the gate, looking up. And I type as I look.

The gate is called the Golden Gate; in the New Testament it is called the Beautiful Gate (Acts 3:2).

It's not the same gate, of course. But it is a gate built at about the same spot as long ago. It is the gate through which Savior Y'shua will enter his city. It is the gate to the Temple Mount facing the Mount of Olives. The Hebrew prophet Zechariah tells us that when he comes again to the earth, Messiah will come first to the Mount of Olives (Zechariah 14:4). He will enter the city from that point. He will establish his kingdom at that time.

Zechariah says, "The LORD will be king over the whole earth. On that day there will be one LORD, and his name the only name" (Zechariah 14:9).

As I look up at the gate that stands today, I am looking at a structure that dates back to the time of the Turkish Sultan Suleiman the Magnificent, who rebuilt the walls of Jerusalem in 1536. But the foundation stones go back further. Back to Turkish, Crusader, and Roman periods. Back to Herod's time. Back to Solomon's time. The gate I see is ancient in its roots. It is one of the sagging gates of Psalm 24.

The gate I see is magnificent. In the last century it was described in this way:

> This is a massive structure, a double gateway, projecting from the eastern wall into the area of the Noble Sanctuary, in which stands the Great Mosque. . . . After the second revolt and total ruin of the Jewish people, Hadrian (136 A.D.) built a new city, which he called Aelia; and . . . he raised a temple to Jupiter on the site of the Temple of Solomon. The style of the Golden Gate appears to refer it to this period. The external front and arches are of Roman origin; and of the interior it is evident that a central row of noble

Corinthian columns and a groined roof, had once formed a stately portico of Roman workmanship! (Robinson & Biblical Researches, *Jerusalem and Surroundings Through the Ages*, Naomi Beecham [Jerusalem: Palphot, 1984], page 9).

There is something strange about this gate, however. It has been walled in! Many years ago the Turks learned that the Jewish and Christian Messiah would enter the Holy City of Jerusalem through this gate.

So they walled it in to keep him out!

How long do you think their stones will hold him back before the King of Glory enters his city to establish his kingdom?

*The gates are his!*

## Our Song

But the song is ours.

As we think of Psalm 24, we find that the singing is ours to do. This is a psalm *of* the Savior Y'shua, but not a song *by* Y'shua.

It is a song for us to sing. One day we will join all creation in singing these words with joy.

Because Y'shua is Lord of Song, he has given *us* a song to sing as well.

But our song is not just the future song of praise when he enters his holy city.

*Our song is now!*

He has given us the song of salvation; it is a new song which he has placed in our mouth. Many will hear, and will fear, and will place their faith in Y'shua.

They will join us, as we join others, in the choirs of the ages in praise to him who is *Lord of Song*.

# PART THREE

# The Songs We Sing to Y'shua

CHAPTER

# 11

## The Beauty
## of Song

**Y**'shua is Lord of Song. But he has given us songs to sing. Our songs are songs of praise to him and to the Father for the gifts of grace we have found in Y'shua.

Have you ever stopped to consider that the center of your Bible is a hymnal? The book of Psalms is a book of music. It was first the music of ancient Israel; now it is the music for all the church to sing, and from which we continue the art of ever making new music to the Lord of Song.

While Psalms is a book of music, only its lyrics have come down to us—no musical notation system has survived. This appears to me to be God's providence. Had we been able to reproduce exactly the singing of ancient Israel, we likely would believe that such a pattern is the only proper way to make music to the Lord. And we would be the poorer for it.

As Yahweh in his mercy hid the burial place of Moses, so he in mercy has hidden the musical forms of the ancient Hebrew people from us. We are too prone to make shrines where we ought to be making progress.

Music lives as music progresses. We are heirs to the treasures of the ages. It all belongs to us because it all belongs to him. All the best music of the ages and cultures of man may be used to praise the Lord of Song.

Music is his. He gives it to us as his gift. We return it to him with joy in worship.

## Praise and Beauty

A lovely psalm that describes the role of music in the life of the believing community begins in this way:

> Sing joyfully to the LORD, you righteous;
>> it is fitting for the upright to praise him.
>> (Psalm 33:1)

This verse pulses with energy. The opening imperative means "to give a ringing shout for joy." The context is music; the mood is exultant praise.

I am attracted especially to the second member of the verse, and to the word the NIV renders "fitting." This Hebrew word, *nā'wâ*, basically means "beautiful." That is, the second member of the verse could read, "praise from the upright is beautiful" (so New King James Bible).

This word *nā'wâ* is used in the Song of Songs to describe a beautiful woman. Her lover says of her that she is beautiful of lips, of face, of form. Each time, he uses the Hebrew word found in our psalm.

The word is also used in the book of Proverbs to describe a negative state of affairs. With the negative element before it, this word describes how unfitting it is for a fool to be wealthy, successful, or honorable.

The word, then, can refer to physical loveliness as well as moral fittingness. In Psalm 33 it describes praise as an *act of beauty*.

When God's people praise him rightly, it is something beautiful they do. They bring beauty to him. And he adds their beauty to the cushion on which rests his throne, for the God of Israel inhabits the praises of his people.

Praise is an act of beauty to God!

## Praise and Music

When we seek to praise him, we are most effective in music. For it is music that may draw the whole body together and give all a sense of participation.

My colleague Gordon Borror loves to train choirs in the service of worship to God. He works with church choirs, seminary choirs, and most notably, an immense choir of gifted singers who perform masterworks of church music each spring.

But Professor Borror insists one choir is more important than any other: This is the congregation as a whole. Congregational singing is more important than the singing of individuals or special groups. Why? In congregational singing all participate; we do not merely observe others praising God by doing the work of ministry in music.

There are godly men and women in the church who have an inadequate and sub-biblical view of music. They think of music as a filler, as a warm-up, as passing time. They think of music as the *preliminary* and the sermon as the *main event*. By this attitude the people become listeners and note takers—well-informed, highly motivated, godly people, to be sure—but with no common outlet for corporate praise of the God they love. This short-circuits the cycle of praise in their life.

> God, give us a biblical center!
> Help us to see Y'shua as Lord of Song, and to see us his people as his singers.
> Give us music; let us give it back to you with wonder and delight!

**Music, Praise, and Art**

The Bible is so balanced; we tend to be so slow in seeing that balance! Listen to the balance in the words that follow:

> Praise Yahweh with the harp;
> make music to him with an instrument of ten strings.
> Sing to him a new song;
> play skillfully with joyful spirit!
> (Psalm 33:2-3, personal translation).

Here is a compressed, biblical statement on music that is balanced and convincing. The poet speaks first of instrumentation. When he calls for the harp, it is for a familiar and common instrument of his day. When he calls for the ten-stringed lyre, it is likely he has in mind a more exotic instrument. In paralleling these words, the poet is using what we call a *merism*, a use of opposites to indicate totality.

He calls both for a common instrument and a more exotic one to indicate that all instruments may be used in the praise of God. Psalm 150, in the spirit of this poem, tries to catalog the instruments of ancient orchestras that might be used to praise God.

In our own day we are embarrassed by riches in the instrumentation God in his providence has allowed to develop. All may be used for him! From the majestic queen of instruments, the pipe organ, to the modern acoustic guitar (whose ancestry may be traced to the time of David!), the instruments are all for us to use.

Today we even have synthesizers capable of special effects that earlier musicians could only dream about. These too are God's gifts.

A friend of mine is a rabbi of a large congregation in our city. Once I asked him why his orthodox Jewish synagogue does not use any instruments. They have a highly trained cantor, choirs, congregational singing; but they have no instruments. Not even a castanet!

He told me, with a twinkle in his eye (surely he knew how I would use this!), his traditional congregation does not use instruments because of their lament for the fall of the temple. He said his people were like their ancestors in ancient Babylon. Out of land, away from temple, they have hung up their instruments on the poplar trees (Psalm 137:2).

"But," the rabbi said, "when the Messiah comes, then we shall use all instruments given to man. And we shall sing in a major key!"

You and I who know Messiah *has* come in Y'shua have every reason in the world—and in heaven!—to praise him with our voices and with all the instruments he in providence has allowed to develop.

## The New Song

The second part of this poetic teaching on music speaks of a new song done with skill and with joy. How balanced all this is!

The call for a new song is not just a desire to throw out

the old hymnals. The best of the old songs will always be new when they are sung with understanding (1 Corinthians 14:15).

The call for a new song is principally a demand for a new appreciation of music and for a freshness of approach to the music we do use. If the psalms really demanded new songs only, there would be no reason for the continued use of the very psalms that make these demands. The whole notion of the canon of psalms would be undermined.

But song is to be new, and that does keep us on the growing edge of music. Music is so varied, so full, so expressive—none of us appreciates all that we might.

I was asked recently to write an article on classical music for a leading Christian monthly magazine. The point of the article, as it was assigned, was to tell evangelical Christian people that they may learn to enjoy classical music in the western tradition as a great gift of God.

One person wrote a letter to the editor complaining strongly about my article. I'm still not sure what article she read! She thought that I was saying that once one became a Christian, there was almost a magical event that makes him love classics (there isn't, and I didn't say there is!). She also thought I was guilty of ethnocentrism by saying Beethoven was so wonderful. She wished me to know that certain aboriginal music is ever more complicated than the music of the old German master.

Whether more complicated means better is debatable, but I will give this to my critic. I will give her ten hours to listen to her aboriginal music if she will give me ten to listen to my Beethoven—and we will both be better!

We will both be the better yet if we leave the one-up-manship behind and join together in a great hymn (her choice!) of praise to God.

If there were never another song written, there would be new music for us all. But God's gifts abound, and his music is everywhere!

## Skill and Joy

Psalm 33 presents balance in the presentation of music as well. It combines what Gordon Borror and I have attempted to describe as the art of worship and the heart of worship. The line begins, "play skillfully"; the manner *does* matter to God! "Just any old thing, if your heart is right," is more often an excuse for laziness than a mode of piety.

But the words continue, "and shout for joy!" Or as I have phrased it, "with a joyful spirit!" An approach to music that is state-of-the-art may lead to professionalism in the worst sense: form over content, external instead of reality. An approach to music that is heart without art is better piety, but has no integrity—no music.

The choirs of David and Solomon were trained choirs. The musicians who performed in the temple were accomplished. Their skill enhanced the people's worship, it didn't detract from it. No one's worship is improved by tolerating sloppy players!

But the state of the heart is basic. Music that is performed well, but with no heart for God, is not an act of worship.

Hence, we strive for the biblical balance:

Sing to him a new song;
　　play skillfully, with joyful spirit!
　　　　(Psalm 33:3).

The most important aspect is as the beginning: It is music done "*to him!*"

## God's Gift
Y'shua is Lord of Song.
　　Music is his gift to us.
　　　　He has made us singers with Y'shua!
As we joy in Y'shua, we shall joy in music.
　　As we learn from Y'shua, we shall respond in music.
　　　　As we worship Y'shua, we do it best in music!
Music is God's gift.

## Subjective/Objective
Many of the psalms of David are what musicians today might call *objective* praise. They speak directly to God of his wonders and excellencies.

Other psalms are more *subjective*, describing what God has done for the believer and emphasizing the believer's response to God.

I think it needs to be stressed that both are biblical models. We tend to react and not to respond. Many feel that too much of today's Christian music is subjective. In distancing themselves from the subjective element of music, some seem to deny its role altogether.

But the Bible presents both, refusing to call one higher or purer than another. The key again is balance.

In technical terms, the objective praise music in the Bible is called *Descriptive Praise*. Psalm 100 is this kind of hymn.

The Bible's more subjective praise music is termed *Declarative Praise*. Here God is praised for what he has done to a particular believer in delivering that person from harm and in instilling a sense of the newness of song to God. An example of this is Psalm 40, a poem we have already studied as a description of the song of Y'shua before he became man.

**My Story**

Let's turn back to that psalm and look at the first words again. I wish to use these subjective words of praise to relate a very personal story.

A British reviewer of one of my earlier books, which I closed with a personal narrative, said that at first he wondered if this were not a very "American thing" to do. Then he said it was a very biblical thing to do, and he thought David would have liked it.

My hope is that not only David, but you, too, will like this story. My deepest prayer is that Y'shua, Lord of Song, will also be pleased.

In the next chapter I present my father's story in the context of the newness of praise that comes in the opening words of Psalm 40, words that fairly scream for regular and personal response.

Constantly I called Yahweh;
 he turned to me and he heard my cry.
He lifted me out of the slimy pit,
 out of mud and mire;
He placed my feet upon a rock,
 and made my steps secure.
  He placed in my mouth a new song,
   a hymn of praise to our God;
  Many will see and fear,
   and will trust in Yahweh.

In the next chapter I will tell you the story of my father, the late Barclay Allen, and how God placed a new song in his mouth.

As you read the story, may you give praise to Y'shua, Lord of Song! And may your praise be a thing of beauty.

CHAPTER
# 12

---

# The Song
# of My
# Father

It was one of those nights one will never forget. Never!

Famed gospel singer Sandi Patti was seated at my right. She had just finished singing, and I had sensed heaven opened as the beauty of her art wrapped my praise and wafted it upward. Her singing in itself made the night one I would not forget.

On my left was a dear college friend who had arranged for my special seat. Next to him was Dr. Billy Graham. This was a night!

Then George Beverly Shea went to the podium to sing just before the sermon by Mr. Graham.

The piano introduction caught me totally by surprise. This my friend had not arranged. This was the Lord's doing, through the action of Mr. Shea.

He began to sing the words of a song that has meant more than life to me:

> I Found a Friend
>     when life seemed not worth living.
> I Found a Friend
>     so tender and forgiving . . .

I looked over to where my wife was seated in the near stands in the stadium in Boise, Idaho. She was weeping. Mr. Graham reached around my friend Carl Johnson, smiled as he touched my arm, and I began weeping also.

This was a song my father had written years ago. Later that night, Mr. Shea told us that he has sung it at every Billy Graham crusade everywhere in the world since 1953.

This is the story of how my father wrote that song.

## Like a Fairy Tale

In some ways my father's early life was like a fairy tale. He was born into a house of music on September 27, 1918. His mother was an accomplished classical pianist and organist. She was also a well-known teacher of music in Denver, where she lived with her husband, Jesse, a barber. They lived in a large home with two grand pianos. My father was born rather late in their life together; they doted on him, their only child.

Dad's mother, Inez Arnold Allen, was an exceptionally dedicated musician. She would practice several hours each day, often rising very early in the morning to maintain her schedule. She would give lessons in the afternoon.

I have only fleeting memories of my grandmother, as she died when I was quite young. I do know that she suffered a stroke at one point that confined her to bed for some weeks when her child was still very young.

During this period, an exceptional thing happened that she related to a reporter for *The Rocky Mountain News*:

> When Barclay was only 14 months old, I was taken ill and was not allowed to see my son for several weeks. At frequent intervals I heard a faint sound which I managed to identify as "Humoresque." This continued for weeks and I was sure that I was dreaming, but imagine my surprise when, after having recovered sufficiently to be permitted to sit up, I one day saw my little son pull himself on the piano bench and very slowly hammer out "Humoresque" with one finger.

## The Fairy Tale Grows

Mother Allen began to pour herself into her talented son. Her great musicianship was a help to him; her excessive doting likely led to emotional dependencies that were to trouble him later in life.

Dad was gifted with perfect pitch, an incredible ear. Roy Olson, a childhood friend five years older than my dad, relates this story. At the age of nine, Roy was taking piano lessons from my grandmother. Little Barclay, then four, might be passing down the hall. He would call out, "No, Roy! The top note should be a B flat, and A flat in the left hand."

At thirteen his prodigy seemed unbounded. One article from those days says:

> Today he directs a 14-piece orchestra at the First Evangelical Church, plays the pipe organ at Simpson Methodist Church, is trumpet soloist in the Highland concert band and a soloist in the senior band and orchestra at Cole (Junior High).

> In addition to playing the violin, trumpet, clarinet, xylophone, piano and organ, Allen has been giving lessons on each of these instruments for four years. He also teaches the viola, cello and saxophone.

## Other Sounds

In the Allen home, Mother "put down the law": Her son would play only classical music.

He began to hear other sounds, the sounds of jazz and swing. Fats Waller and Teddy Wilson became his new musical idols, an uneasy alliance with Chopin and Beethoven.

In a *Valley Times* (Van Nuys, California) news article some years later, Dad reflected:

> I was 15 before I dared play jazz and popular music in Mom's presence. Anything not classical was strictly taboo. But she finally gave in to a little popular music ... and even allowed her students to taste it.

She did not know that it would be in popular music that he would make his mark—and break her heart.

## Marriage and Radio

After high school, Dad married Vantoria Hahn, his sweetheart from Manual Arts High in 1937. He went to Lamont College of Music for a short time, but then took a job with radio station KFEL.

In those days radio stations which broadcast recorded music had to have live studio musicians on staff for a certain number of hours each day. This made work for musicians. Dad became staff pianist and organist, and was then given a thirteen-piece string group for radio shows.

Dad would also take club dates whenever the opportunities came—even if he would have to learn a new instrument to do so. Once he was asked to play an accordion at a supper club for a weekend. He rented an instrument on Wednesday and learned how to play it on Thursday. By Saturday he had the people at the club convinced that this was his principal instrument. He gave a superb performance on a new instrument which he never really liked or played again!

From KFEL Dad moved to KLZ and formed some relationships that would last his lifetime.

He got star treatment not only in the press (we have pages of clippings), but also in the station by his pals. On one early morning program, he would arrive "just on time." In fact, they would hold the doors open for him and he would make a production of sliding right onto the piano bench as the red light would come on announcing that the program had begun.

Friends tell the same story. By his actions he would make people furious. But they could not stay mad once he began to play! He would win them back time and again by the magic of his fingers on the keyboard. Everyone I have talked with tells me it would be hard to overestimate his musicianship; he had a great gift.

## To Hollywood

Dad's firm goal in life was to direct a big dance band. To further that goal, we moved to Southern California shortly after the death of Dad's mother and the end of World War II.

In 1945 I was four and my sister Peggy was two.

Before Dad could work in California as a musician, he had to establish a residence for six months to meet union regulations. He could not afford to be idle for six months, so he took a temporary job as a "scab." The place was a pit on Pico Boulevard in downtown Los Angeles.

Dad did not know how rough the neighborhood was. He had Mom ride the bus to come hear the show one night. The band leader, Jimmy Medina, on seeing Mom, asked, "Who is the woman?" Dad responded, "That's my wife."

To Jimmy this was no joke. "Quick, quick!" he said. "Get her up on the stand." Medina insisted that Mom sit on the piano bench with Dad the rest of the night. It was not a nice place!

With his six months established, Dad got his union card and left dives like that forever. That is not to say that he was out of the slimy pits, however. That would take some time yet.

## Radio and Recordings

Even with talent it is never easy to make it big in the music business. Friends and breaks are also needed. Dad had both.

Friends from Denver who had moved to the coast helped Dad get a job as musical director at KLAC with a staff orchestra. The announcers at the time were Dick Haynes ("at the reins") and Bob McLaughlin.

McLaughlin and Dad formed an independent recording company called Van-Es, after the names of their wives, Vantoria and Esther. Some thirty sides were released on the label with Dad's quartet, called *The Rhythm Four*. This group would later become the nucleus of his big band. The players were Stan Black, guitar, Sid Fridkin, bass, and Merle Mahone, drums.

Dad then landed a job with Kay Kyser as pianist for the band on its popular national broadcast. Roc Hillman was instrumental in getting Dad this job. Roc and Dad began a long association in composition. Roc was a guitar player who had worked with Jimmy Dorsey and Bing Crosby in the thirties. His great standard is "My Devotion" (1942).

It was also with Kyser that Dad met Jane Russell and became her accompanist and life-long friend.

### "Por Que?" to "Cumana"

The story of how Barclay Allen wrote his greatest hit is one of last-minute insight. The quartet was in a recording session at the McGregor Studios. They were making a series of twenty- minute transcriptions. At the time there was an ASCAP strike, so they could not use a tune licensed by them. They needed one more song to fill out a side— and the whole side had to be done in one take.

In five minutes, Dad put together the basic structure of a fast *samba*. The tune itself was not long enough to fill the allotted time they needed. The musicians inserted a *montuna*, a middle section where the players would fake it. This is what makes the song! Then they had to have a title after they finished recording. They exhausted their Spanish with "Por Que?"

Months later Dad's lyricist Roc Hillman improved on that by coming up with "Cumana." He was poring over a new Britannica Atlas, and he picked out a city name in Venezuela. This song became the door to Dad's fame. Ironically, years later ASCAP wrote me to ask if I could locate the music for "Por Que?" They had no official record of its copyright. I had no idea what they were talking about until I got the story from Roc and Merle Mahone.

### Big Time

Dad's big break came when he received a call from Freddy Martin. Freddy Martin's pianist, Murry Arnold—like Jack Fina before him—was leaving to start his own band. Would Dad be interested in joining the Martin band?

Would he? Martin's band was made to order for Barclay Allen. Freddy was at the peak of his "concerto period." He featured a classically trained pianist who could play dance rhythms with flair. This *was* Dad.

"Cumana" was recorded by Freddy's band, featuring Barclay Allen at the piano. Total sales for "Cumana" went over a million. Now a standard, "Cumana" has been recorded perhaps two score times from bands as diverse as Stan Kenton and Lawrence Welk.

Other recordings with Martin's band featuring the piano stylings of Barclay Allen included "Sabre Dance Boogie," "After You've Gone," "Jungle Rhumba," and many others. Allen and Hillman compositions joined this listing: "The New Look," "It Began in Havana," "Barclay's Boogie," "Beginner Boogie," and others.

Through recordings, road trips, and the home stand of the Martin band at the Cocoanut Grove in the Ambassador Hotel, Los Angeles—Dad's name was becoming well known. Rumor had it that he was the highest paid side man in the music business.

## And Did He Play

Long-time radio broadcaster Chuck Benedict reminisces on these glory days:

> I guess there never was a hotel-style band which permitted a pianist so much freedom as Freddy permitted your Dad. Barclay was a master of the brilliant-but-tasty frills. His own "signature" was in all his free-play opportunities, and the piano became a bigger part of the band than ever before or since. Your Dad was at his best.

The inevitable happened, and all too quickly. Dad had long wanted to front his own band. Despite a gracious offer from Freddy for a long-term contract, Dad quit to go on his own.

Freddy Martin is dead now. But I spoke to him on the night after he celebrated his fiftieth anniversary in the music business. He had me write down these words:

> Barclay Allen was a brilliant musician and he had a touch at the piano that was most extraordinary. In addition, he was a wonderful composer.

Such praise was often coming from a gracious Freddy Martin. It came as well from critical reviewers. A writer for The Billboard called him "a showstopper" and one from

*Variety* "an excellent performer." A writer for the *Boston Herald* said:

> A young man of decided talent. . . . Star of show
> . . . solid rhythm, sure technique. Pianist of stun-
> ning virtuosity . . . the marvel's name is Barclay
> Allen, and what he does with such contrasting
> things as "Bumble Boogie" and the various con-
> certi is not of the world.

## A Band of His Own

Now he was on his own. Early in 1948 Dad gathered together some fine musicians, developed new charts, and
began rehearsals for his new band. He had a fine personal
promotion agent in Carson Harris and M.C.A. The band
opened at Ciro's in Hollywood on 5 March 1948. No sleazy
dive on Pico anymore. Ciro's was high class, the big time.

Peggy Lee was the headliner that night. My mother remembers shaking hands with Perry Como. Frank Sinatra
was there. The band was booked for six weeks, but stayed
ten.

## On the Road

After the opening at Ciro's, the band began what was to
become an eighteen-month road trip. The first booking was
in Dad's home town of Denver at the Elitch's Gardens. At
the same time, "Cumana" was being performed in a sym-
phonic setting by D'Artega at the famed Carnegie Hall in
New York.

The band went from Denver to a number of major
hotels across the country: the Chase in St. Louis, the Syra-
cuse, the Peabody in Memphis, and the Palmer House in
Chicago. Some stays were quite long: fifteen weeks at the
Chase, twenty-three at the Palmer House. Billed as "Music
Magic," the band received strong reviews.

Each bandsman traveled by private car with his wife.
Several also had children. The band was somewhat innovative in that they functioned as a cooperative. They all believed that the band would do well.

I have many memories of that long road trip. I remember reading lessons with my mother on a hotel mez-

zanine. My sister and I had a royal pillow fight at the Chase. A kind maid helped to clean up the feathers that were flying everywhere. I remember running up to the bandstand once at Elitch's and helping Dad hand out autographs to fans. I remember mornings in parks, hot afternoons in movie theaters, lots of driving, long hotel stays, all meals eaten out, and missing home terribly.

## The Rough Road

The life of a musician in a dance band on the road in those days was unnatural. The hours were late, the adulation of the fans deceptive, the booze and broads all too available. The romance of such a life was quickly given the lie.

Not all the rough spots were because of long road trips, one-nighters, rained-out fairs, and the like. Many of the rough spots came from Dad's drinking. He was soon an alcoholic. Sometimes he would be late to arrive on the stand. Since the band featured his playing, the absence of the leader was not easy to cover. Some of the players began to lose confidence in his leadership.

While Dad was fighting these problems, I was led to the Savior in a remarkable way. My mother must have had a spiritual craving for a long time. I remember her reading to me and Peggy from a Bible story book in our hotel rooms.

While we were at the Chase Hotel, the band singer prevailed on my mother to take me and my sister to hear a woman who taught from the Bible for children. This vocalist thought it was too bad that children of the bandsmen were not under any spiritual teaching.

For the first time in my life, at age seven, I was given a clear and effectual presentation of the gospel of the Lord Jesus by that woman in her little class. She used a flannelgraph board and presented the call of the Savior beautifully.

She taught us a prayer, but said to wait until evening before praying it. "Make sure you mean business with God," she said.

That night, as my parents were arguing about my dad's drinking, I became the first in our family to know the Lord.

As my life was coming together, the lives of my parents were coming apart. In the long months of travel with two children and a husband who was neglectful and uncaring, my mother decided she would begin a new life on her own. We left the band and spent a good deal of time with friends in Denver. Then we made our way back to California. My mother wanted a life of her own.

The band continued its road trip, making its way back to the west coast. In Boise, Dad and one of the musicians were arrested for drunken driving. They were over two hours late to the band stand that night.

Passing through short stays in Portland and Grant's Pass, Oregon, the band came to Santa Cruz, where they added a troupe of dancers and singers for a big production, "A Salute to Gershwin." Stuart Wade, a fine vocalist with Freddy Martin, joined the band. They went to the Mark Hopkins in San Francisco, the el Rancho in Sacramento, and then the Cal-Neva in Lake Tahoe. The plan was to proceed from there to Las Vegas, where the band and the troupe were to play the Flamingo.

**Tragedy**

Tragedy struck while the band was at the Cal-Neva Lodge on the north shore of Lake Tahoe. The eighteenth of August was a Thursday. Dad had been drinking a great deal that day. After the show that night, he drove off by himself to go to Reno. Eyes heavy, he fell asleep at the wheel. He failed to make a turn on the mountain highway. The car plunged down an eighteen-foot embankment. Dad was thrown partially out of the car, but lay pinned in the wreckage.

He lay unconscious for five and one-half hours, as determined by his broken watch. He was found the next morning by a man and woman who were fishing along the Truckee River, near where the car had come to rest.

Dad was taken to the Washoe Medical Center in Reno, where examinations disclosed the very serious nature of his injuries. He had suffered great loss of blood, irreparable cellular damage, a broken neck, and a pinched spinal column.

By God's grace, there was a skilled surgeon on the staff. He had experience with severe spinal injuries from the winter and summer sports in the area.

Nonetheless, Dad nearly died three times during those first days. My mother came to the hospital as soon as she heard of his accident. She recalls with horror the time she saw Dad upside down in the Stryker Frame: blue in the face and nearly dead.

A couple of years ago I received an unsolicited letter from a woman who is nationally known for her work with Stonecroft Ministries, Mrs. Millie Stamm. She tells how she heard the news of Dad's accident on the radio:

> As I listened to the news, such a burden came on my heart that I dropped to my knees asking God to spare his life until someone could talk to him about his relationship to Jesus Christ.

Perhaps it was her prayers and the prayers of godly people like Mrs. Stamm that kept my father alive during those early days of his hospitalization.

Dad reacted to his accident with terror and rage. When he regained consciousness, he became aware of a patient in the next bed who had lost both legs in a boating accident. In shock, Dad accused Mom of having had his legs amputated.

## How Could God?

My dad had never had much time for the things of the Lord. He was a classic example of one who believed that God had given him a gift, but that he owed God nothing more than to use the gift without giving God glory.

Now he learned he would never play the piano again. He was paralyzed from the neck down. It was irreversible. He would never walk again. He would never play again.

His thoughts of God were filled with rage: How could God have allowed such a thing to happen?

At the time of his accident, Dad was just thirty years old.

## Supporting Friends

Many people came to aid my parents during those early weeks and months of my Dad's injury. Addie Olson flew from Denver at her own expense to volunteer as a private duty nurse for Dad at the hospital in Reno. She was the only nurse who would not let him get away with nastiness. He was filled with rage, and he tried to take it out on anyone near.

Hospital and doctor bills mounted quickly. Many of Dad's friends in the music business did benefits to raise funds for his care. These included Stan Kenton, Freddy Martin, Frank Sinatra, and others. A recording was made of "Cumana" some time later with a vocal rendering by Jane Russell, Connie Haines, and Beryl Davis. Bob Hope sent a letter to disk jockeys all over the country asking that this record be played. Freddy was particularly helpful in terms of royalties during those years.

Help came in others ways as well. Many disk jockeys followed the lead of Nick Kinny of the New York *Daily Mirror* in asking that fans write Dad notes of encouragement. Thousands of cards and letters came to the St. Joseph's Hospital in Burbank, where Dad had been transferred.

Personal help came in new friends as well. Wally and Clara Gammel did hundreds of hours of practical help around the home for Dad's care.

In December a particularly distinctive book of personally autographed glossy photos of leading singers, musicians, and entertainment personalities was presented to Dad by Freddy Martin. This book is a family treasure. Among my favorite inscriptions is this:

> Dear Barc. When you get back in action again and you need a trombone player, I'm available. I read, fake, improvise and am willing to travel. Hurry up, Barc. We all miss you. Sincerely,
>
> Tommy Dorsey

## Enter Pastor Hammer

Many people came to help. But none was able to help where Dad hurt the most. He had not lived well, but he had played well. Now he would never play again. The loss of music in his life ate away at him.

Almost immediately after Dad came to St. Joseph's, the Reverend Norman Hammer came into the life of our family. Merle Mahone remembers his first view of Hammer. The pastor had on a gray suit, red tie, and chartreuse socks—"looking all the world like a third sax player." He could not believe this was a preacher.

Hammer tried to see my dad right after he was admitted to the hospital. Dad flew into another rage. He wanted nothing to do with a preacher. Pastor took Mom out for coffee and began to soothe her spirit.

People who had known my mom say she was a woman looking for spiritual reality in her life. She believed from the beginning that there was a purpose in Dad's living after his accident. "He was meant to live," she would insist.

One time Dad was very ill in the hospital. He was in a complete coma and had been so for over twenty-four hours. His temperature was between 105 and 106 degrees. Pastor and Mom prayed beside his bed. Pastor prayed that if Dad were not ready to meet the King of glory, that he would be given more life to prepare himself. Right in the middle of the prayer, Dad came out of the coma and began to speak to my mother.

"He was meant to live." These strong words were used of God to lead my mother to further inquiry. She began attending an adult instruction class at the church where Pastor Hammer ministered. During one of the class sessions, without anyone expressly leading her, my mother found the truth of the gospel. She accepted Christ as her Savior. Soon after that, Peggy came to the Lord.

But the musician in our home wanted nothing to do with our song.

## The Hammer

Pastor Hammer kept coming to see Dad, even though he was often met by rebuff. Hammer had a great sense of humor. He would tell jokes that were mildly amusing, but would laugh and laugh. Others would join in the joy of his laughter.

Sometimes Dad would hear that great laugh coming down the hospital hall. He would ask a nurse nearby to pull the curtain around his bed. "Tell him I'm in therapy; tell him I'm dead—but don't tell him I'm here."

Pastor, with a flourish, would pull aside the curtain and say, "Hi, Barc!"

Weeks passed. Then months.

Dad shriveled from about 200 pounds to a low of 87. He had decided to die. Life was simply not worth living. He had constant pain. He had no music. He did not wish to live. He had no use for religion, either; for him that was just for squares. It was strictly "C" melody.

Pastor kept coming. He and Mom kept praying for my Dad.

Dad reached a very low point.

A dramatic scene took place at my father's bedside one day when he felt that he was going to die. Mother and Pastor Hammer were called to the hospital; Dad wanted to say goodbye.

My mother went in first. Dad told her that he loved her. She asked why he was trying so hard to leave. He responded, "It's the pain. I can't live with the daily pain. And I can't live without any hope of music."

The Pastor came in as Mom went out to the hall.

I have heard Hammer tell this story many times. He would always say this was not his usual approach, but this was no usual moment. The Spirit of God prompted him to say some things he "never learned in seminary."

Pastor came into my dad's room, leaned gently against the bed, and said: "If you really knew where you were going, you wouldn't be in such a hurry to get there."

Gasp.

Hammer then said, "Perhaps I should bring in your wife and the two of us will say 'octagon'."

"Octagon? What's that?"

Hammer responded, "That's goodbye from two squares! Perhaps you should just kick off, and I will get your widow and orphans straightened out."

Dad's response was incredulous: "What right have you

170

to throw your weight around, talking to a dying man like this?"

"If you are still around tomorrow, I'll answer that and any other question you might have." With that, Pastor spun on his heel and left the room.

My father was kept alive that night by sheer rage.

For the first time since his accident he had his rage working for him instead of against him. He wanted to tell off that pastor who had spoken so harshly to him.

Pastor came back.

Not once, but again and again.

He came back with the Word of God.

My dad's list of questions came again and again.

Pastor first won Dad's confidence, then his friendship, then his heart.

Finally, after many visits, Hammer was able to lead my father to the place where he accepted the Lord Jesus Christ as his Savior.

And at long last, my dad had learned the new song!

## The Song Is New

Remember the words of Psalm 40:3?

> He placed in my mouth a new song
>   a hymn of praise to our God;
> Many will see and fear,
>   and will trust in Yahweh.

This was the story of my father's turning from darkness to light. God gave him a new song to sing, a whole new reason for music.

As time passed, my father gained strength and was able to get into a wheelchair. As he gained strength, he was even able to play the piano again. The level of his paralysis was in the high chest area; it did not permanently affect his arms.

He was never able to play as he had before the accident, of course. But he did learn to play again.

In one arduous venture, Dad followed the lead of injured musician Les Paul. He tried to make a recording using a concept that was then new: overdubbing. He used five separate sound tracks. He played the Hammond organ on one, the celeste on another, and two different piano tracks. Roc Hillman played the guitar on the fifth. In a very complex arrangement that called for great precision, he recorded two songs: "After You've Gone" and "Cherokee." For each song he spent eighteen hours in the studio, working for an hour and then resting for thirty minutes. Longtime friend Roc Hillman was joined by Jane Russell in encouragement. *Newsweek* ran a two-page article on how the record was made and that Barclay Allen was playing piano again.

## "I Found a Friend"

But another kind of music came from the new Barclay in the spring of 1953. He called his dear friend Norm Hammer to hear his testimony in song in the new hymn, "I Found a Friend."

The lyrics were written by Dad's long-time collaborator, Roc Hillman. This time Roc did not just look on a map to find a place name that would fit a Latin song!

Roc wanted very much to capture the conversion story of Dad in a way that would speak of his special story, and yet speak to a broad audience in reverence and praise to God. Roc told me that at first he did not think he was up to doing it. He flew to New York with Dad's music to present the idea to another well-known lyricist.

But he did not let go of the song. On the way back on the plane, Roc prayed about his task and the words came. He says to this day that these words were "definitely God-given."

This was the song that George Beverly Shea sang that night as I sat between Billy Graham and Sandi Patti. In these words came the flood of memories of my father and how he came to love Y'shua.

Here are the words:

> I Found a Friend when life seemed not worth living
> I Found a Friend so tender and forgiving,
> I can't conceive how such a thing could be,
> That Jesus cares for even me.

Each day each year my faith in Him is growing.
He's ever near, His love is overflowing.
I have no fear, my worldly cares are few.
I can depend on Him to see me through.
I Found a Friend and He is your friend too.

When Bev Shea had finished singing, Mr. Graham went to the pulpit. He turned to where Mr. Shea was sitting and said, "When you sang 'I Found a Friend' tonight, you had no idea that the son of the composer was seated right beside me."

At that, Shea got up and made his way across the platform, gave me a bear-hug, and invited us to dinner with him later.

## And Still He Sings

Dad lived seventeen years after his accident. He died on 26 November 1966 of a heart attack, a long-term result of the accident. I wish I could say that he never wavered in his singing of the new song. I cannot do that. Even with his perfect pitch, Dad did not always keep in tune in his new life in the Savior.

But he did do a number of things well in recordings, personal appearances, a television film, and in his witness to the work of the Savior in his life.

When Dad was forty-eight, God called him home. Now he was ready.

Today, my sister Peggy is a minister's wife, living with her family in Washington state.

My mother lives in Southern California; she attends Grace Community Church in Panorama City, where John MacArthur is pastor.

A life lived fully for Christ is a better thing than a dramatic story where only broken pieces are given to the Lord. Yet my dad did leave a legacy of joy. Chuck Benedict wrote me these words:

> One of the rationales that makes me know that in truth there is a heaven is that there is something so very fantastic about the God-given talent of a man like Barclay. Yet, life here is so short,

and it is absolutely impossible that a loving God who created such beautiful talents, and also created the love for such talent, would let such great talent just die, unfulfilled.... In many ways, his success is to be only in heaven.

Then he adds,

Yet, when I think back to my life as it touched his, I believe he was a great success. Look at his legacy to those who did get to know him.

Here are the last words of Dad's song:

Because He came my soul will live in glory.
I'll praise His name, and tell my Savior's story.
What friend so true would give his all for you?
I Found a Friend and life began anew.
I'm sure you'll find that He is your friend too.

You see, David had it right all along:

He put a new song in my mouth,
 a hymn of praise to our God!

# 13

# So
# Let's Join
# the Song!

**Y**'shua is Lord of Song. From the moments before his incarnation, he had a song of praise to sing to the Father, saying, "Here I am, I have come . . . I desire to do your will, O my God" (Psalm 40:7-8). Throughout his life he pointed to the whole of the Scriptures, but particularly to the book of Psalms. It was especially in his Passion that the psalms took on their special function as the libretto for his suffering and the songs of praise for his victory over death.

Because Y'shua is Lord of Song, his people have renewed reasons to praise him in song. We learn to praise him as we come to salvation. We continue to praise him as we grow in faith and become part of the worshiping community.

God loves the praise of his people in song. One of the psalms begins this way:

> *Hallelu Yah!*
> How very good it is to sing praises to our God,
> How pleasant and beautiful his praise!
> (Psalm 147:1, personal translation).

All of heaven is filled with his praises. When we sing to Y'shua in songs of praise, we join the choirs of angels and all his heavenly hosts (Psalm 148:2).

The music of praise pervades the Scriptures. It is even found in the book of Revelation. Time and again that book of judgment and vision is punctuated with music of praise to God and his Christ. One of the great hymns in Revelation is called the song of Moses the servant of God and the song of the Lamb. Here is that song:

> Great and marvelous are your deeds,
>> Lord God Almighty.
> Just and true are your ways,
>> King of the ages.
> Who will not fear you, O Lord,
>> and bring glory to your name?
> For you alone are holy.
> All nations will come
>> and worship before you,
> for your righteous acts have been revealed.
>> (Revelation 15:3-5).

## So Let Us Sing!

So let us join in song in praise of Yahweh, who has done such great things for us! Let us join in song in praise of the Lamb who is worthy! Let us join in song to our God, who has placed a new song in our hearts!

Isaac Watts said it this way:

> Come let us join our cheerful songs
> With angels round the throne;
> Ten thousand thousand are their tongues,
> But all their joys are one.
>
> "Worthy is the Lamb that died," they cry,
> "To be exalted thus."
> "Worthy the lamb," our lips reply,
> "For He was slain for us."
>
> Let all that dwell above the sky,
> And air, and earth, and seas,
> conspire to lift Thy glories high,
> And speak Thine endless praise.

## SO LET'S JOIN THE SONG!

The whole creation join in one
To bless the sacred NAME
Of Him that sits upon the throne,
And to adore the Lamb.

*So let us sing!*

Y'shua the Lamb is Lord of Song!